www.wadsworth.com

wadsworth.com is the World Wide Web site for Wadsworth Publishing Company and is your direct source to dozens of online resources.

At *wadsworth.com* you can find out about supplements, demonstration software, and student resources. You can also send e-mail to many of our authors and preview new publications and exciting new technologies.

wadsworth.com
Changing the way the world learns®

Developing Your School Counseling Program

A Handbook for Systemic Planning

Zark VanZandt
University of Southern Maine, Gorham

Jo Hayslip
Career Transitions

BROOKS/COLE
™
THOMSON LEARNING

Australia • Canada • Mexico • Singapore • Spain
United Kingdom • United States

BROOKS/COLE

THOMSON LEARNING

Counseling Editor: Julie Martinez
Editorial Assistant: Marin Plank
Marketing Manager: Caroline Concilla
Project Editor: Matt Stevens, Teri Hyde
Print Buyer: Barbara Britton
Permissions Editor: Joohee Lee

Production Service: Gustafson Graphics
Copy Editor: Linda Ireland
Cover Designer: Bill Stanton
Cover Images: Courtesy of Corbis Images
Compositor: Gustafson Graphics
Printer: The P. A. Hutchison Company

Printed in the United States of America
4 5 6 7   06 05

Library of Congress Cataloging-in-Publication Data
VanZandt, Zark.
    Developing your school counseling program:
a handbook for systemic planning/Zark VanZandt, Jo Hayslip
        p. cm.
    Includes bibliographical references and index.
    ISBN 0-534-56295-7
        1. Educational counseling—United States—Handbooks, manuals, etc. I. Hayslip, Jo. II. Title.

LB1027.5 .V2965 2000
371.4'0973—dc21   00-037870

Wadsworth/Thomson Learning
10 Davis Drive
Belmont, CA 94002-3098
USA

For more information about our products, contact us:
Thomson Learning Academic Resource Center
1-800-423-0563
http://www.wadsworth.com

International Headquarters
Thomson Learning
International Division
290 Harbor Drive, 2nd Floor
Stamford, CT 06902-7477
USA

UK/Europe/Middle East/South Africa
Thomson Learning
Berkshire House
168-173 High Holborn
London WC1V 7AA
United Kingdom

Asia
Thomson Learning
60 Albert Street, #15-01
Albert Complex
Singapore 189969

Canada
Nelson Thomson Learning
1120 Birchmount Road
Toronto, Ontario M1K 5G4
Canada

Contents

Preface

We, the coauthors, have worked together on a number of projects since 1975. We have written this handbook because we both felt a need for functional training materials for school counselors. We have taught a counselor education course—School Counseling Programs and Services—in our respective colleges. We have tried a number of textbooks over the years and have found them to be wonderful theoretical models, but we found two audiences that need practical hands-on learning materials: (1) our students, who are about to move into school guidance programs, and (2) practicing school counselors and program directors who want to change their programs but do not know how.

We have organized this handbook as a process-oriented opportunity for counselors to learn by application. Activities are provided to allow the reader to practice school counseling program management in the relatively safe learning environment of the college classroom or a school counseling team planning session. Students can play the roles of counselor, student, parent, or administrator. Practicing counselors who use this handbook can actually involve these individuals in the change process. The handbook is based on a logical developmental approach. When you have completed the handbook, you will be prepared to organize and reorganize school counseling programs on a developmental, comprehensive basis.

Because of the importance of linking theory to practice, we have continued to use traditional primary texts in our courses, and we use this handbook as a supplemental text. School counseling programs should also rely on theoretical frameworks to guide their change process.

The 1990s were a turning point for a renewed emphasis on first determining the needs of the students and then bringing together the resources to meet these needs. Throughout the handbook, you are asked to develop your own model for delivering a comprehensive guidance and counseling program to all the students in a given school. We provide some models that we know well, such as the New Hampshire Comprehensive Guidance and Counseling Program and the Maine Comprehensive Guidance Program, as examples to help you conceptualize your own model; but we also believe it is essential to encourage creativity and fresh ideas.

Throughout this adventure we ask you to keep in mind the human factor. Sometimes school counselors become so involved in the guidance process that they lose sight of the complexities of human relationships and human development. We are people working with other people; as human beings we all have only ourselves and our expertise to offer in helping others to grow to the fullest development possible. Counselors must lead their programs in a human-directed manner, with the aim of encouraging everyone in the system to become actively involved in delivering a comprehensive developmental guidance and counseling program.

NEW DEVELOPMENTS

Readers who have used the previous edition of this handbook, *Your Comprehensive School Guidance and Counseling Program: A Handbook of Practical Activities,* published by Addison, Wesley, Longman in 1994, will note significant changes in terms of updated material and the format. Activities have been moved closer to their text descriptions. We have also made the handbook more user-friendly by including spaces for writing about activities directly within the text.

Chapter 1, "Creating Frameworks for Program Success," is expanded to include activities from recent writings in Stephen Covey's *7 Habits of Highly Effective People* and Peter Senge's *The Fifth Discipline.* The application of these current resources serves to enhance comprehensive developmental programs.

Chapter 2, "Working as a Team," is a new chapter. As we worked with students and with school counseling program planning teams, we found that we needed to place greater emphasis on the human factor. The comprehensive developmental school counseling model will be effective only if those individuals who are involved first learn to work together as a team. Activities and strategies are presented to ensure that group process is utilized and that team building is done.

Chapter 3, "Conceptualizing the Program," takes the team through the process of seeing the big picture and all of its components by emphasizing flowcharting, a systems approach. Participants first inspect our flowchart development and then, working in groups, develop their own flowchart and its accompanying plan of action.

Chapter 4, "Examining Program Models," explains in detail the Missouri model as designed by Gysbers, and an adaptation of this model by counselors in New Hampshire. Since the publication of the first edition of this handbook, several additional models have been developed: the National Standards for School Counseling Programs, the National Career Development Guidelines, and the Secretaries' Commission on Achieving Necessary Skills. These models are presented for your consideration.

Chapter 5, "Determining Program Priorities and Focus," includes several new activities (for example, a community assessment and a more detailed needs assessment). The first of two school board presentations is also included in this chapter.

Chapter 6, "Building Your Curriculum," is brand new. Scope and sequence, examples of instructional formats, samples and practice lesson plans, and a list of commercial curriculum resources are offered to assist you in creating your own comprehensive developmental curriculum.

Chapter 7, "Assigning Responsibilities," requires that you continue your creative thinking as you prepare to deliver your comprehensive developmental school counseling program. We ask you to "take a risk" by developing and presenting a staff development workshop. We also ask your team to plot a time line for putting your program into operation.

Chapter 8, "Organizing Program Support," refers back to Chapter 4, "Examining Program Models," and forward to Appendices C, "ASCA Position Statement: The School Counselor and Developmental Guidance," and E, "ASCA Ethical Standards for School

Counselors," and then asks you to gather additional policies and procedures as you seek support from your administration and advisory committee. Budget and resource development continue to be an integral part of this chapter.

Chapter 9, "Developing Public Awareness and Support," is a new perspective on public relations. We have also provided a peek into one Internet listserv with its accompanying public awareness/public relations information.

Chapter 10, "Establishing Program Leadership and Supervision," has been expanded to include a conceptual framework for counselor supervision.

Chapter 11, "Ensuring Professional Development" (formerly Chapter 9), includes a new dimension—the new activities align with the ASCA Ethical Standards (Appendix E) as well as Covey's *7 Habits of Highly Effective People*. We have also added a challenge to the counselor to become a change agent and to take a risk by developing and presenting a staff development workshop.

In *Chapter 12*, "Conducting Program Evaluation" (formerly Chapter 10), in addition to a school counselor performance appraisal instrument, we have added a sample program evaluation and a student competency evaluation.

Chapter 13, "Humanizing Technology," is brand new and reflects the thinking of one of our reviewers, who noted a gap in our efforts to bring this book up-to-date.

Chapter 14, "Synthesis" (formerly Chapter 11), as with the first edition, wraps up the entire process with your school board presentation. We heartily suggest that if these procedures are followed in this manner, you will triumph with a successful, comprehensive developmental school counseling program.

ACKNOWLEDGMENTS

Writing, and rewriting, this handbook has been fun! The two of us became more and more excited about this project as it continued to evolve and as we included more people in making the dream a reality. As with any adventure of this type, so many people were helpful in bringing the project to fruition that we would like to acknowledge their contributions.

We appreciate the work of Isabel Myers and Katherine Briggs (and all of their protégés who keep refining the use of the Myers-Briggs Type Indicator). While working on this book, we have recognized the complementary strengths of an Extraverted, Intuitive, Thinking, Judging (Jo) and an Extraverted, Sensing, Thinking, Perceiving (Zark) partnership; and we used our knowledge of the Myers-Briggs typologies to assist us in seeing the big picture and its parts. We had to process our own process, and in doing so, we had a great time rediscovering how much we enjoy writing together.

Two very special people have accompanied us on our mission to spread the word about comprehensive school guidance programs. James V. Carr, Vocational Guidance Consultant, New Hampshire Department of Education, and Nancy Perry, Guidance Consultant, Maine Department of Education, have been leaders in the movement to change school counseling from reactive services to proactive programs. We appreciate their wisdom, experience, and friendship.

Jo's husband, Ellwyn, has provided steady support from the early stages of the project, and his creative contributions to the graphic layout and design of the handbook have helped in the conceptualization of the paradigm. Ellwyn has a long history of lending his artistic talents in support of counselors; his latest contribution, *A Handbook of Practical Activities to Guide You to Your Career in Crafts*, is in a limited printing and available in high school libraries throughout the New England states.

Zark's wife, Kitty, has not only been supportive of the many hours spent in creating this handbook but has also contributed several very important activities that work for her in her work as a director of guidance. In several instances, she has tried out an activity in her "real world" of guidance and returned with valuable information.

We are most appreciative of the contributions of our students at Plymouth State College and the University of Southern Maine. They have participated in the experiment to move to a model of cooperative learning in the counselor education classroom, and they have provided both the challenge and the reinforcement that has shaped the final product. Their questions have been insightful; their suggestions have been incorporated at all levels because they make so much sense; and their excitement about being counselors and their dedication to their training have been inspirational. We cannot wait for all of them to be out there in the schools, reshaping the vision and image of school counseling.

We would like to thank the following reviewers for their helpful comments and suggestions on the second edition: Deborah Barleib, Kutztown University; Nick Colangelo, The University of Iowa; James O. Fuller, Indiana Wesleyan University; Donna A. Henderson, Wake Forest University; V. Skip Holmgren, Sonoma State University; and Carolyn Stone, University of North Florida.

It has been a delightful experience working with a talented and dedicated group of editors at Brooks/Cole Thomson Learning. In particular, we would like to acknowledge the patience and professionalism of the production team headed by Matthew Stevens and Teri Hyde, the outstanding copyediting provided by Linda Ireland of Gustafson Graphics, and the competent and conscientious production management by Sara Dovre Wudali of Gustafson Graphics. A special thank you is extended to Julie Martinez, who encouraged the concept and orchestrated the development of this project.

Certainly, we want to acknowledge the cumulative contributions of thousands of superintendents, principals, specialists, parents, teachers, counselors, community leaders, colleagues, and leaders in the professional organizations who have helped to mold our thinking and perspective over the years. But, most of all, we want to thank the students in kindergarten through twelfth grade with whom we have worked—because after all these years, we still believe that counseling is the most noble of professions, and the students are the reason the job is so exciting and rewarding. It is because of the students that we want to help create school counseling programs that are the pride of the school system. They deserve only the best.

A FINAL INSTRUCTION/OBSERVATION

We have each field-tested this handbook in Organization of School Counseling programs. We are aware that any work can be improved, and we look forward to your input after you have used this handbook for one semester. Thank you in advance for your comments and feedback.

Zark VanZandt   Jo Hayslip
University of Southern Maine   Career Transitions
Gorham, Maine   Concord, New Hampshire

Introduction

HOW TO USE THIS HANDBOOK

This handbook is designed to teach you about the practical aspects of managing a school counseling program. It is not filled with extensive theory and philosophy. It is concerned with promoting useful methods of helping counselors to be more productive and accountable, and with challenging counselors to continually refine their own delivery systems.

In regard to importance and relevance to the needs of both counselors and clients, a handbook on the management of school counseling programs is essential if the practicing counselor is to maximize resources and services so that theory and process can flourish. The interdependent nature of the various facets of the counseling profession requires that the counselor seriously address the demands of a well-managed program.

The handbook is based upon multidimensional models of guidance and counseling program management. It presents a number of models, but it also gives you the opportunity to develop your own. Experience suggests that the school guidance and counseling programs with the best reputations are those with well-thought-out program designs complemented by competent staff and leaders. Although some programs focus upon specific services to meet the needs of targeted populations, the outstanding programs see the big picture and meet the needs of all the students.

The ability to perceive, respond to, and manage the whole spectrum of counseling is what this handbook is all about. With a multidimensional approach to guidance and counseling program management as a framework, the handbook identifies, describes, and analyzes the components (little pictures) of the total management scheme (big picture), then brings the entire experience back into focus for the counselor to synthesize and put into practical use (the new big picture).

AUDIENCE

This handbook is designed for two primary audiences: counselors in training and counselors already working in schools. Counselor education programs typically offer a course called "Organization and Administration of Guidance and Counseling Programs." The authors' investigation of counselor education programs reveals that increasing numbers of programs are recognizing the significance of such a course. We believe that this material should be required of all counselor education students who plan to work within a public school setting, and we believe this handbook will complement any assigned text. The second audience, the practicing school counselors, is more specifically identified as those practicing counselors who are serious about updating their programs to align with national models of excellence and to meet the ever-changing needs of students in a complex global society. Guidance directors or counselor supervisors who are interested in restructuring their school counseling programs to meet the needs of this changing world are included in this latter group. Guidance directors receive little or no training in how to manage a school counseling program, but this handbook addresses that concern by offering a site-based management model. Counselors working together as cooperative learning teams can create quality programs that break the mold from traditional school counseling services.

Counselors in any setting must understand the goals and services of the total program in order to complement those services. Being a good "team player" is essential for realizing the total impact a program can provide for its clientele. If counselors understand the purposes, complexity, and interrelatedness of all aspects of a school counseling program, they may become more accepting of the less-than-engaging functions of the position—or they will learn to delegate some of these functions to those in positions to handle them more appropriately. These not-so-glamorous functions exist in all counseling settings, so the management skills may be put to use wherever efficient and comprehensive counseling programs are sought.

Counselors who are the sole proprietors of a regional office or elementary school cannot escape the need for management skills even though they may not see themselves as directly part of a team. In fact, these individuals may be the most needy, for they are responsible for *everything* that happens in their work setting. If they fail to see the big picture, and limit their involvement to just certain obligatory administrative duties, a comprehensive program cannot become a reality. A careful, objective look at the counseling profession suggests that we all need good management and leadership skills.

SPECIAL NOTE TO COURSE INSTRUCTORS AND PROGRAM MANAGERS

We have included a variety of activities to help counselors and counselors-to-be to actively participate in the practical application of counseling program management skills. As instructors or program managers, you will need to make choices about which activities should be used in large groups, small groups, or left to the discretion of the individual learner. For example, a course instructor may choose to have an entire class do the needs assessment activity in Chapter 5 to make sure everyone understands how it is done, but may assign the public awareness activities in Chapter 9 to small groups. Likewise, the program manager may decide that the entire K-12 counseling staff needs to generate the "why" questions in Chapter 1, but may assign the grant-writing activity in Chapter 8 to a special subcommittee that has expressed interest in identifying outside funding sources. Careful selection of the appropriate activities will set the tone for the program management issues that require the greatest emphasis if the groups are to be successful.

FOCUS

We are living in an age of accountability. Counselors, like all other professionals, must respond to the demand for accountability. This handbook offers school counselors and counselor supervisors a framework in which to (1) view the total functioning of the school counseling program and (2) perceive the various roles and functions that must be integrated into the total program for the counseling services to be truly accountable.

The handbook will also foster skills and knowledge in the areas of program development and supervision of school counseling programs. These competencies are not solely the domain of program directors and supervisors; they are areas in which all counseling practitioners must demonstrate both skills and positive attitudes if school counseling programs are to make the best use of their resources. By making a conscious effort to integrate their individual preferences with all other functions of the counseling program, counselors can help to develop a well-rounded and well-synthesized program.

If school counselors are to help students reach their maximum potential, they need to model how they reach their own maximum performance as counselors. This handbook is designed to empower school counselors to create the most effective programs, to assemble the best available resources, and to demonstrate their feelings of worth as counselors. This is an ambitious endeavor, but we have faith that all counselors truly want to be the best that they can be. We also believe that if counselors are open to change, they can empower themselves. The strategies and resources provided here will enhance that empowerment.

METHOD

Both authors believe in the power of cooperative learning. In recent years, schools have found a depth and richness of learning results from students working cooperatively to develop products or procedures: group members' strengths surface and are expressed; group pressure urges some members to new heights of performance, while other members learn how to encourage, motivate, and assert themselves; written and verbal communication skills are enhanced; team building and risk-taking can be fostered and nurtured; shared responsibility becomes an acceptable norm; and a more holistic perspective leads to results of higher quality.

Listening to lectures on rare occasions can be scintillating; however, we believe that learning by doing can be a more empowering experience. Therefore, this handbook is designed with cooperative learning in mind. Most activities in this handbook are designed for small groups; and since we believe that as much can be gained from the process itself as from the final product, a means of "processing" the group experience is included in the last chapter of the book.

REFLECTIONS PAGES

At the end of each chapter, we have placed reflection questions. Please use these as an opportunity to reflect upon your work, personally and as a group. If you write down your thoughts and feelings as you progress through your tasks, you will be able to return to these pages as you begin to assemble your final process and product. Although you are not required to share the personal notes that you accumulate, you might find these of valuable assistance to your group. Keep these notes faithfully, and they will serve you well.

Chapter 1

Creating Frameworks for Program Success

As counselor educators, one of our favorite questions to ask students is "Why?" We realize that such a question seems like sacrilege to those who have been admonished not to ask "why" when counseling clients. There are thousands—maybe millions—of why questions counselors could ask. We will get to some of them later. For a moment, however, we want you to ponder the question of why. We believe that why is one of the most critical words in a counselor's vocabulary if used with conviction and skill, so we are going to tell you why you should be asking why.

When you were a child, did you become frustrated if you asked a question like "Why do I have to go to school?" and you got a reply such as "Just because . . ." or "Because it is good for you"? Did you vow then that when you were an adult and children asked you that kind of question, you would give them a much better answer?

DEVELOPING A RATIONALE

An unfortunate phenomenon evolves for many of us as we become adults—we find ourselves repeating the behavior that was modeled for us long ago. Now, when people have the audacity to challenge us with questions like "Why do we need more counselors?," we find ourselves at a loss to provide truly substantive responses that will make the questioners become wide-eyed and truly receptive to our arguments.

Through the 1960s and early 1970s, schools were rarely challenged about the need for counselors—at the high school level, at least. The United States and the former Soviet Union were waging a battle for superiority in space, and the National Defense Education Act (NDEA) had been established to make our schools more competitive. Many counselors' positions were created with the intent of getting more students interested in taking math and science courses. Once the trend shifted toward school counselors in the elementary grades, however, skeptics surfaced. Many wondered why "therapists" were needed in the schools; others questioned why students should be prepared for college so early. Trying to educate the public to extend its perceptions of school counseling beyond scheduling or getting students into college has been one of the major challenges of the profession.

In the 1970s and 1980s, *accountability* became a buzzword. Some counselors, however, especially those who had been trained to use the therapeutic model, tried to argue that counseling should not be subjected to the demands for accountability because it is a process, not a product. After all, how can you quantify insight and motivation? Recessions and deficits, however, brought many important issues into focus. Counselors began to see that accountability was not just a passing whim; it was here to stay.

From a developmental perspective, counselors who respond to the call for accountability because it is imposed upon them by a higher authority might be placed in the early stages of professional growth—what one might call the preoperations stage, to borrow from the wisdom of Piaget (1969). At this early level, external locus of control imposes its rules and sanctions on those who either need or allow themselves to be led by others. Counselors who assume more and more responsibility for developing their own programs and for demonstrating their worth to a critical public seem to move to a level of identity in which intrinsic motivators predominate. At this level of "formal operations," counselors possess more of an internal locus of control, and realize they are the ones who are primarily responsible for the success and acceptance of their programs. By embracing the concept of accountability, counselors then begin to assume tasks, promote change, and provide leadership. At the highest levels of this developmental continuum, counselors value the concept and nature of accountability and incorporate it into their daily performance in an almost automatic manner.

Activity 1.1 Asking Why

1. Take a few moments to think about some of the why questions that are surfacing in your own mind as you think about the role of the school counselor and your work in the schools. We have generated a list of why questions for you to ponder, but do not read our list until you have worked together in small groups to generate your own questions. Use the following space to list what you consider to be the most thought-provoking questions generated by your group.

    a.
    b.
    c.
    d.
    e.
    f.
    g.
    h.
    i.
    j.
    k.
    l.
    m.
    n.

2. Following is the beginning of our list of why questions. Look them over and compare them with the list that your group generated. Feel free to add your own questions. The list is by no means exhaustive.

    a. Why should we hire another counselor?
    b. Why are there so many kids in need of individual counseling?
    c. Why should we be doing classroom guidance when so many kids are in need of individual counseling?
    d. Why are teachers reluctant to let counselors in their classrooms?
    e. Why do administrators not provide more support to counseling programs?

f. Why are counseling positions some of the first to be cut when there is a budget crisis?

g. Why cannot counselors do what they enjoy most—and forget the rest?

h. Why did I want to become a counselor in the first place?

i. Why do so many counselors resist being good managers of their programs?

j. Why do we need comprehensive K–12 developmental school counseling programs?

k. Why

l. Why

m. Why

n. Why

3. What generalized messages can be gleaned from this exercise? What other questions need to be asked?

Now, you would probably appreciate it if we would just give you the answers to these questions so that you could get on with your life, but we cannot make it that easy! Besides, there is no one right answer to each of those questions—nor will there be any simple reasons for most of the challenging questions that face counselors as they develop, implement, and revise their programs. The answers to the questions may vary because of circumstances, personalities, socioeconomic needs, structural boundaries, philosophies, theoretical persuasion, personal preferences, resources, higher-level thinking, creativity, education and training, politics, and economics, to name just a few of the variables. Obviously, neither the questions nor the answers are simple ones.

We do believe, however, that students should spend some time trying to generate their own responses to these questions (and their own questions). Herein lies the significance of generating such a list: *In seeking and formulating the answers, you establish the purpose for your own behavior as a counselor.* Purposeful behavior is time well spent. If counselors do not know why they are taking on certain responsibilities or performing certain tasks, their motivation will more than likely be at a minimum. Furthermore, if in the process of seeking answers to the why questions, counselors cannot rationalize their (or the program's) behavior, then they should abandon the tasks. With the thousands of things a counselor can be doing to fill a day's schedule, we certainly do not need to be taking on tasks for which there is very little purpose.

DEFINING ACCOUNTABILITY

There are many definitions of *accountability*. We offer one definition that sets the tone for much of what follows in this handbook. We would like you to approach this definition more as a dissection activity in a biology class than as a dictionary activity in an English class, since looking at the various components of the definition should help you appreciate the complexity of the concept and seek the meaning and significance of its parts:

Accountability is a condition / in which meaningful information / about program needs / and accomplishments / is made available / to those who are responsible for / or affected by the program / and avenues are accessible / for creating changes. (Wysong, 1973)

We will now isolate separate phrases from this definition to highlight the various responsibilities to which counselors need to attend.

Accountability as a Condition

A condition is a state of existence created by various factors; it is pervasive rather than situational or isolated. A counselor cannot sit down one day and comply with accountability as if it were a task. Creating the condition of accountability takes time and thought; it entails conceptualizing and planning so that all those involved can agree on the factors that promote accountability and the kinds of responsibilities that must be assumed for those factors to be addressed.

Meaningful Information

What makes information meaningful? What kinds of information are people looking for when they demand accountability? Are they looking for quantitative data that impresses them with facts and figures? Do they value subjective comments? Will they understand the context in which any given accountability report is delivered? Will they be so critical of the way you present your program that they will not be able to look at your program's accomplishments? By identifying those who will receive the information, we should be able to see it from their perspective so that we can address their conceptualization of meaningfulness. If we understand the consumers of such information, we will more clearly understand how to make it meaningful.

Program Needs

Identifying the areas of need that should be addressed in a school counseling program is a major task. Despite years of training as a counselor, no one should rely solely on professional judgment in determining the priorities of the program. Seeking input from others is an important part of accountability and requires some fairly sophisticated skills. Chapter 5 will lead you to appreciate the significance, complexity, and challenges of creating valid needs assessment procedures.

Program Accomplishments

We need to promote our own program—to blow our own horn! We cannot wait around for everyone to recognize all the good things we do; others are busy keeping up with all the good things they are doing. Bragging about ourselves, however, runs contrary to all those admonitions that we were given as children. Nonetheless, if we recognize the need to let people know that we have been successful in addressing the needs we have identified, then we must learn to brag with humility. Public awareness and support is such an important topic that we have devoted an entire chapter (Chapter 9) to the subject.

Availability

If we spend countless hours, days, and weeks compiling information about program needs and accomplishments, and the information sits on a shelf or hides in the recesses of a file drawer, we have wasted our time. We need to share the information and we need to give considerable thought to the most appropriate ways to make it available so that people really understand it and use it.

Responsibility

We certainly need to feel responsible for our own programs. Does the responsibility end there, though? If we think more globally, we recognize that school principals feel responsible for all that goes on in their buildings, that school superintendents feel responsible for all the education programs in their districts, and that school board members feel responsible for representing the public's best interests. In a well-integrated program, we need to foster a sense of responsibility on the part of classroom teachers, librarians, support staff, and others who contribute regularly to the objectives of our program. We can even make a case for Toni Taxpayer, who is wondering whether her tax money is being spent for a worthwhile cause. We will stop there, since we are sure you get the point. It is always important to remember, however, that those who feel responsible will most likely be more committed and involved in the program.

Beneficiaries

In looking at the people who benefit from our school counseling programs, we need once again to think globally. The students are the primary beneficiaries of our services, but parents and teachers also need to be included as groups who benefit from our various roles. In a more indirect way, the community has much to gain from a strong guidance program. Is the same information meaningful to each of these groups?

Accessible Avenues

We need to be creative in exploring opportunities for seeking and sharing information about school counseling program needs and accomplishments. Looking beyond the traditional end-of-the-year report, we should think about the different ways in which we receive information that pique our curiosity or motivate us in some way, and then use that awareness to create avenues of communication.

Change

Rarely does change take place in a hurry. If we expect change to take place within the context of accountable school counseling programs, we need to keep in mind all the facets of accountability and the many ways that change can take place. Steady improvement should be the kind of change we seek.

Activity 1.2 Personalizing Accountability

Now, without looking at what you just read (no peeking!), jot down the most important things you want to remember about accountability. Do not be limited by the definitions given above; personalize the meaning of *accountability* so that you create a definition of the term that you can use.

Next, working in your small groups and without looking at the definition that we have given, try to put together a "consensus" definition of *accountability*.

COUNSELOR EFFECTIVENESS

We recognize that some people get upset when schools are compared to businesses. We are *not* in this business for profit—or *are we*?! It all depends on your perspective. If we keep our focus on how *students* profit from their experience in schools, then we are certainly in the business of providing programs of the highest quality. If you are one of those who resist advice from the business sector, we would like to caution you to not "throw out the baby with the bath water." In the past few years the business sector has certainly learned some powerful lessons from the human services field. With that caution in mind, we would like to share some powerful lessons from two individuals, Stephen Covey and Peter Senge, who have had a significant influence on the way people view their work and their lives.

Lessons from Covey

In his national best-seller, *The 7 Habits of Highly Effective People*, Stephen Covey articulates some basic concepts of effectiveness that make perfect sense in the context of designing and implementing comprehensive developmental school counseling programs. What is especially gratifying is the knowledge that most counselors have received advanced training in these areas of effectiveness; therefore, the challenge is to learn how to apply and integrate these already existing skills in a framework of program effectiveness.

Covey describes how paradigms are models, theories, perceptions, assumptions, or frames of reference; and he stresses the importance of understanding how "paradigm shifts" are needed if people are to change their behavior. That is, we are never going to change our ways unless we see why we should change and how we should change. Covey suggested that paradigms are powerful because they create the lens through which we see the world. Being open to new and better paradigms will help counselors pursue the models and plans that reach students in more effective ways. Following are summaries of the seven habits and explanations of how they apply to the school counselor's professional responsibilities.

Habit #1: Be Proactive

This first "habit" is the essential issue that differentiates comprehensive developmental school counseling programs from those that are more traditional in their delivery of services. Traditional programs are primarily *reactive;* comprehensive developmental programs are *proactive*.

We often hear from counselor education students who, with the best of intentions, state that when they become counselors they are going to have an open-door policy that lets students know that they are there when they need them. On the surface, that statement sounds warm and inviting. On the other hand, it is also sending the message that counselors will react to students' needs instead of anticipating and addressing many of the developmental issues that students face so the students can be empowered to understand and cope with these issues as they arise.

Covey explains that people with a reactive focus put much of their energy into working within a "circle of concern." Here again we find people with the best of intentions responding to the complexities and injustices of various systems and encounters; and in the process, they become burned out and overwhelmed by the enormous burden they carry. Proactive people, on the other hand, focus their efforts on the "circle of influence," attending to the matters over which they have some control. Within this paradigm, proactive people seek ways to increase the size of their circle of influence.

Whether a school counseling program evolves as one that is proactive or reactive is a matter of philosophy. We are not talking Socrates or Descartes here—we are talking about basic belief systems regarding the needs of students. Every counselor in a school counseling program needs to be a part of the discussion about what the underlying philosophy is that provides the foundation for an effective program.

Activity 1.3 Time to Philosophize

Discuss the following questions in small groups.

1. Is an "open-door policy" essential for a student in crisis? Why or why not?

2. Can a school program be both developmental and reactive?

3. What do all students "need" from a school counseling program?

4. Should all counselors in a school system philosophically agree with one another about how the program should operate?   Why or why not?

Habit #2: Begin with the End in Mind

Since this second habit is based on the principles of personal leadership and management, it plays a significant role in how well counselors can put together a quality program. Too often, in schools where a director of guidance is the recognized head of the school counseling department, the rest of the counselors relinquish all responsibility for both leadership and management to that individual. In effective programs, *all* counselors assume responsibility for "doing the right things" and for "doing things right." This collective responsibility happens when there is a collective vision about what the program should look like. Covey suggests that both imagination and conscience are characteristics that are important contributors to potential leadership. The same is true for program leadership. Counselors need to imagine the best possible school counseling program and use the highest principles of their profession to create a visionary model of excellence.

According to Covey, the most effective way to begin with the end in mind is to create a mission statement. In Chapter 5 of this book, we have you further explore how the mission statement helps shape the collective vision of what your school counseling program should look like. As Covey points out, "an organizational mission statement—one that truly reflects the deep shared vision and values of everyone within the organization—creates a great unity and tremendous commitment" (Covey, 1989, p. 143).

Habit #3: Put First Things First

A day in the life of a reactive school counselor can be downright exhausting. Of course, a day in the life of a proactive counselor can be exhausting, too, but there is a difference in the kind of energy that has been expended. Covey reminds us that this third habit of putting first things first is not so much about managing time as about managing ourselves. Counselors employing this habit put most of their time and energy into managing the priorities of a proactive program.

A time management matrix is provided by Covey to help us recognize whether the activities in which we are engaged fall into one of four quadrants:

Quadrant 1. Activities that are urgent and important
Quadrant 2. Activities that are important but not urgent
Quadrant 3. Activities that are urgent but not important
Quadrant 4. Activities that are neither urgent nor important

To many, the first impression would be to spend the most time and energy in the first "quadrant" of the matrix, attending to those matters that are both urgent and important. This is how reactive counselors operate. Covey recommends that we become opportunity-minded instead of problem-minded, and put our energy into a schedule that represents balance, perspective, self-discipline, and a focus on minimizing crises. Prevention takes precedence over putting out fires. Looking ahead to Chapters 6 and 7, we will help you to create programs that put first things first.

Habit #4: Think Win/Win

This fourth habit represents an area in schools in which counselors should shine. Thinking win/win means operating according to a conceptual paradigm that constantly seeks mutual benefit in all human interactions. Teaching peer mediation or conflict resolution skills to students is a well-respected and very rewarding part of the job for many school counselors. School counselors also often find themselves in the middle of rifts between teachers and students, students and their parents, administrators and teachers, and so on. Win/win is a philosophy, not a technique; yet, some of the skills we employ as counselors are reflective of our philosophy that things can be worked out if we learn to listen to one another and think creatively and with conscience.

Counselors can serve as role models for the win/win perspective in asserting their roles as change agents. Our counseling skills become transferable skills as we develop our habits of interpersonal leadership. You will work in much more depth with this concept in Chapter 10, Establishing Program Leadership and Supervision.

Activity 1.4   Trained to Be Winners

Covey asserts that there are five interdependent dimensions of life that embrace the principles of win/win. For each of the following five dimensions, cite courses or specific techniques within your counseling training or staff development training that have helped you develop the win/win principles that can guide your practice.

1. Character (that is, integrity, maturity, and an abundance mentality)

   Example: the core conditions of counseling

   _____

   _____

2. Relationships

   _____

   _____

   _____

3. Agreements (giving definition and direction to our interactions)

   _____

   _____

   _____

4. Supportive systems

   _____

   _____

   _____

5. Processes (actual methods for working toward win/win solutions)

   _____

   _____

   _____

Both the win/win philosophy and the next habit illustrate how counselors have unique training that prepares them for leadership roles as part of an interdependent team of educators.

Habit #5: Seek First to Understand, Then to Be Understood

One of the things that is so fascinating about this habit is that the general population struggles most with the first part and school counselors struggle most with the second part. Because of our unique training, school counselors spend countless hours trying to listen empathically to the needs of students, parents, teachers, and administrators. Absolutely nothing in this book will encourage you to operate in any other way. Our only advice is that you give this skill away on a regular basis, and then learn to balance your listening skills with high-level advocacy skills.

Counselors need to be role models of empathic communication. In doing so, we allow others to hear themselves and recognize their needs. We also need to teach listening skills—through classroom instruction, inservice education, parent classes, newsletters, or other means—so that those with whom we work are empowered to get their needs met. If you ask a room full of people (with the exception of a group of counselors or communications majors) whether they have ever had formal instruction in how to listen, chances are great that only a small handful of individuals will raise their hands. We need to increase the percentages.

In the context of this book, the fifth habit has tremendous significance. In Chapter 5, we will demonstrate how conducting a needs assessment is one of the ultimate forms of empathic listening. Such powerful empathy requires listening with our ears, eyes, minds, and hearts. Later, in Chapter 9, we will stress the second half of this habit as we discuss how the development of public awareness and support depends on the program being well understood.

Habit #6: Synergize

Simply defined, synergy is that which exists when the total is greater than the sum of its parts. Unfortunately, too many school counseling programs lack the synergy that could make them great—or make their schools great—because there are too many independent parts functioning without a clear picture of what the "whole" could or should be. Chapter 2 talks about synergy as a by-product of cooperative teamwork. However, this entire book is about school counselors working to develop the synergy needed for quality school counseling programs. Even though the last chapter of the book is called "Synthesis," it was a temptation to call it "Synergy." Feel free to change the title as your efforts lead to synergy.

Habit #7: Sharpen the Saw

Covey talks about the physical, social/emotional, spiritual, and mental renewals that are necessary for individuals to continually strengthen the other habits. He illustrates the concept of renewal with an example of a person exhausting himself by using a dull saw to try to saw down a tree, and refusing to take the time to sharpen the saw because he is too busy sawing. Do you know anyone like this?

If you are a graduate student learning how to be a school counselor, the seventh habit is one that should guide your practice *after* you have completed the exercises in this book. If you are a practicing school counselor, this book is designed to be a means of sharpening your saw. Chapter 11 also helps you contemplate the significance of your renewal efforts.

Covey's paradigm suggests that as individuals gain skills in applying each of the seven habits, they move through levels of maturity in contributing to effectiveness. The early habits help us move out of a stage of dependence toward more independence and personal mastery, then the later habits move us to even higher levels of interdependence. School counseling programs that are effective function within an interdependent framework.

Activity 1.5 Habitual Thinking

Even though this chapter has provided only cursory attention to Covey's seven habits, this is a good time to introduce a formative evaluation that will help you reflect on your own sense of mastery of the habits of effectiveness. Use the self-assessment as an opportunity to target the areas covered in this book where you may really need to sharpen the saw.

The 7 Habits of Highly Effective Counselors

A Self-Assessment

Directions: For each statement below, rate your level of understanding, commitment to, and application of the concept being described, as it relates to your work as a school counselor. A score of 7 represents the highest level of investment in that concept, while a rating of 1 represents a minimal level of investment. Be prepared to explain or justify your rating to a colleague.

	Low						High

1. Be Proactive
   Comments:

   1 2 3 4 5 6 7

2. Begin with the End in Mind
   Comments:

   1 2 3 4 5 6 7

3. Put First Things First
   Comments:

   1 2 3 4 5 6 7

4. Think Win/Win
   Comments:

   1 2 3 4 5 6 7

5. Seek First to Understand, Then to Be Understood
   Comments:

   1 2 3 4 5 6 7

6. Synergize
   Comments:

   1 2 3 4 5 6 7

7. Sharpen the Saw
   Comments:

   1 2 3 4 5 6 7

Where I see myself on the developmental effectiveness continuum:

Dependence			Independence		Interdependence	
1	2	3	4	5	6	7

Lessons from Senge

Peter Senge's book has an intriguing title, *The Fifth Discipline: The Art and Practice of the Learning Organization*. It makes you wonder about the first four disciplines—as well as the fifth! As the core disciplines are outlined here, you will see that they are wonderful complements to Covey's habits and are fundamental to creating frameworks for program success. There are challenges here for both the individual counselor and the entire counseling staff.

Core Discipline #1: Personal Mastery

In this first discipline, Senge stresses that organizations learn only through individuals who learn. He cautions, however, that individual learning does not guarantee organizational learning. As a discipline, personal mastery embodies two underlying movements: (1) continually clarifying what is important to us, and (2) continually learning how to see current reality more clearly. Schools and school counseling programs provide countless examples of how personal mastery and teams learning (or not learning) together contribute to the quality and effectiveness of those institutions. An integral part of personal mastery is linked to personal vision. Senge reminds us that vision is different from purpose. In the context of comprehensive school counseling programs, defining our purpose relates to answering the why questions in Activity 1.1; our vision relates to what we want the ideal program to look like.

Activity 1.6   Visioning

In the space provided, list some words or phrases that reflect your personal vision of what a quality school counseling program should be. Consider the people delivering the program, the facilities and resources, the services provided, and the image and reputation of the program.

Keep in mind as you move through the exercises in this book that others' visions of the ideal school counseling program may be different from or similar to your own, but the collective vision can evolve only from all the individuals associated with the program pondering their own personal mastery and vision.

Core Discipline #2: Mental Models

Senge's second discipline stresses the significance of "mental models" in shaping how we think and act—in both our personal and professional lives. Mental models determine how we "see" the world—from the simple generalizations and assumptions we make to the complex theories to which we align ourselves; therefore, our behavior is a reflection of our belief systems. Counselors should be able to recognize a cognitive-behavioral perspective to this second discipline.

Senge asserts that a leader's effectiveness is related both to the continual improvement of that person's mental models, as well as to his or her contributions to others' mental models. Since one of the important messages in this book is the idea that *all school counselors are leaders, we try to provide models by which you can improve your* effectiveness as a leader. Chapter 4 in particular helps you explore some school counseling models that may be helpful in pursuing your vision of the quality program that you outlined in Activity 1.6.

Core Discipline #3: Shared Vision

Shared visions emerge from personal visions. The first discipline is the bedrock for this discipline. According to Senge, leaders need to share their personal visions and empathically listen to (or "see") the visions of others. The more group members can merge and refine their personal visions into a shared vision, the more they will be committed to and invested in the program's efforts. The challenge of this book is to get you to work in teams that can create a shared vision of a quality school counseling program.

Core Discipline #4: Team Learning

We agree that team learning lays the foundational framework for a group of counselors and related service providers to create high-quality counseling programs and then to maintain them. Such discipline does not come automatically, however. Learning teams must learn how to learn together. Chapter 2 discusses the significance and the complexity of team focus.

The Fifth Discipline: Systems Thinking

The cornerstone of a learning organization, according to Senge (and Hayslip and VanZandt, as well), is systemic thinking. In its simplest language, systemic thinking means that the whole is greater than the sum of its parts. That simple explanation belies its profound complexity and its elusiveness.

This book could be titled *Get the Picture,* as a metaphor for systemic thinking. School counselors who use systemic thinking are able to see the "big picture." They see both the full landscape and all the small, beautiful snapshots that make up that landscape: the composition of the major objects in the picture, the texture of the medium, the wonder that can be found in a blade of grass or the shadow of a tree, the emotions generated by the images, the impact of the picture on its viewers, the inherent flaws, the manner in which the frame complements the picture, how the picture reflects the artist's style, whether other pictures on the wall look good next to this one, and the people who pass by this picture because they are not attracted to it for whatever reason. All these things are part of the systemic nature of a single picture, as is the pride of the parents who, comparing their child's picture to those of all the other first graders, think that their child's picture is the best of the show! Systemic thinking provides a context for thinking and behaving in interconnected ways—at many different levels.

Senge provides eleven "laws" of systemic thinking. We will share the titles of a few of those laws here to whet your appetite and to challenge your thinking about the complexity of systems thinking:

- The easy way out usually leads back in.
- Faster is slower.
- Cause and effect are not closely related in time and space.
- Dividing an elephant in half does not produce two small elephants. (This is our favorite!)

If you are sufficiently confused by these titles, then you are where we want you to be.

Activity 1.7   Applying the Fifth Discipline

With a reminder that the easy way out is to leave an item blank, write responses to each of the following questions.

1. How might "the easy way out leads back in" apply to the way a person pursues the reading of this book?

2. What are some other euphemisms, laws, or "truths" you have heard that are similar to "faster is slower"?

   "Slow + steady wins the race"

3. What are some critical issues in schools that have been "years in the making" (for example, students with substance abuse problems)?

   - homophobic behaviors
   - harassment issues

4. In what ways is an elephant a good metaphor for a comprehensive school counseling program?

Throughout this book you will find several reminders and activities that will help you explore some of Senge's laws, and by then you will have gained an appreciation of the complexity and significance of systemic thinking. We hope you will return to these laws after you have finished the activities in this book to see if you more fully understand their importance. And if you get hooked on systemic thinking, we hope you will pursue the rest of Senge's laws on your own.

We hope some of the messages and activities in this chapter have provided you with some insight into your own purposeful behavior as a school counselor. School counselors must provide leadership in building schools that are learning organizations. A quotation from Senge summarizes the responsibilities all counselors must share:

> In a learning organization, leaders are . . . responsible for building organizations where people continually expand their capabilities to understand complexity, clarify vision, and improve shared mental models . . . that is, they are responsible for learning. . . . The ability of people to be natural leaders . . . is the by-product of a lifetime of effort—effort to develop conceptual and communication skills, to reflect on personal values and to align personal behavior with values, to learn how to listen, and to appreciate others and others' ideas. (Senge, 1990, pp. 340, 359)

We hope you get the picture (the big picture, as well as the parts).

Summary

In this chapter, we have given the "why" of this handbook. In subsequent chapters, we will help you with the "how." Keep in mind that this handbook is intended to assist you in applying the theory and practice that you will learn from textbooks and supplementary readings. We are attempting to help you conceptualize comprehensive developmental school guidance and counseling programs. This handbook is a blueprint to enable you, the prospective or practicing counselor, to try out some major concepts and to put them into their appropriate perspectives.

References

Covey, S. R. (1989). *The 7 habits of highly successful people.* New York: Simon and Schuster.

Piaget, J. (1969). *The mechanisms of perception.* (G. N. Seagrim, Trans.). New York: Basic Books.

Senge, P. (1990). *The fifth discipline: The art & practice of the learning organization.* New York: Currency Doubleday.

Wysong, E. (1973). Accountability: Foibled fable or solution. *Impact, 2,* 34–37.

Reflections on Chapter 1

1. What was it like to work in a small group?

2. What challenged you most in your "why" activity?

3. What challenged you most in your accountability activity?

4. How do you feel about your role in the group?

5. What questions do you have for yourself, your group members, or your instructor?

6. How do you feel about the importance of the topic of accountability for your preparation?

7. Notes:

 **Chapter 2**

Working as a Team

THE HUMAN FACTOR

Have you ever seen a program that looked really great on paper but fell flat because of the way it was run? To avoid that situation, we offer some sage advice about the balance between management skills and people skills. Outstanding planning and implementation strategies may be rendered useless by inattention to the dynamics of what we refer to as the human factor. People invested in the success of a school counseling program must work to create a cooperative and inviting atmosphere within the school for personnel, parents, community members, and, most important, students. Human skills and an awareness of the human condition are essential ingredients in the overall development of the counseling program, the successful implementation of the many assigned responsibilities, and the direct delivery of counseling and consultation interventions.

The nature of the profession requires counselors to be attuned to individual differences among clients, and also to be aware of the differences among staff personnel and members of the public with whom counselors work. Counselors also must be honest and genuine in examining their own biases and issues that interfere with their ability to be totally objective and empathic. By understanding the issues that people bring to both the therapeutic and management aspects of the counseling program, counselors can become sensitive to the types of communication that will be necessary to encourage receptivity and foster progress.

This chapter examines the concept of teamwork and provides activities to help you see the many applications of teamwork in the overall operation of an effective school counseling program. Because cooperative learning is the recommended mode of delivery for the lessons in this book, teamwork is stressed as the foundation for making cooperative learning a viable process.

Activity 2.1 Exploring the Human Factor

Individually, explore the significance of the human factor in the overall functioning of a successful school counseling program. List some examples of how attention or inattention to the human factor has affected school counseling programs you have observed.

Share the examples in a small group. Create a consensus statement about the significance of the human factor in contributing to the success of the school counseling program.

Start with the Individual

Most counselor education programs require at least some course work in the area referred to by the Council for the Accreditation of Counseling and Related Education Programs (CACREP) as social and psychological foundations. An awareness of the basic tenets of sociology, plus a firm grounding in developmental psychology (as well as other psychological theories), is considered basic to the development of counseling skills. Understanding people and how they seem to function, both individually and in groups, will be the daily challenge for each and every counselor for the rest of her or his professional life. Cooperative learning groups provide an excellent learning laboratory for exploring this application of social and psychological foundations.

The most important human factor in an effective program is the counselor's personality. This is not to say there is one "counselor personality." On the contrary, the counseling profession needs diverse and unique personalities. But all counseling professionals must be committed to continual self-examination and ever-changing self-knowledge. It is critical that counselors know what works for them individually, stylistically, theoretically, and emotionally, in order to be effective.

Sometimes we receive valuable feedback through instruments like the Myers-Briggs Type Indicator (MBTI) (Myers & Briggs, 1992) and the 16 Personality Factor Inventory (16PFI) (Cattell & IPAT Staff, 1991). Such investigations can be enlightening. For example, if a counselor discovers that she is a strong I (Introvert) on the MBTI, she may better understand why classroom guidance responsibilities seem so challenging. With this knowledge, she may work harder to be more extraverted *in the classroom* to facilitate the motivation of students and to reach her goals.

The most challenging and sometimes most intimidating kind of feedback comes from friends and coworkers. They can be affirming in sharing perceptions of your best traits and behaviors, but if they are honest and candid, they will also point out those personal traits and behaviors that work to your disadvantage. Hearing similar comments from several people should help you form an accurate picture of how you are perceived. You can then use this information in positive ways to maximize your strengths and minimize your weaknesses.

Another example is warranted here. A counselor went to three associates and asked them to list his most positive attributes and then to be very honest and give him some feedback about his personal traits or habits that bothered them. He reassured them that he welcomed their criticism because he was trying to improve his image with students and the faculty. When he received the feedback, he was flattered by the many positive things his colleagues had to say about him but was surprised that two of his associates mentioned the clothes he wore as being his greatest deficit. Even the third associate confirmed that the way he dressed might negatively affect the way he would be perceived by students in particular. He was made aware that his clothes sometimes did not match and that when he wore white socks to school, the students made jokes about it. As a result, the counselor bought a book about men's fashions. Later, however, he confided to a colleague that he really did not like the fashions he saw in the book, and besides, he could not afford such clothes with his salary. The colleague decided to spend a Saturday at the local mall with this counselor to point out the basic rules of selecting clothes and to suggest some other alterations in his professional appearance. After changing the way he dressed, the counselor began to feel more confident about how he was perceived by his students and his peers. He realized that, even though it was a little disconcerting to have people tell him that he did not dress well, he was glad they had been candid enough to help him change in a positive way.

Of course, all the feedback that we receive cannot be as tangible or as nonthreatening as discovering that we need a new wardrobe. If we really believe in the importance of the human factor in the success of our school counseling programs, however, we need to be open-minded and receptive to feedback from others.

Activity 2.2 First Impressions

1. Choose one other member of your class or group and spend a maximum of ten minutes each describing what you perceive to be the major problems with today's school counseling programs. To help you think about what you are going to say, write down some of your key points before starting the conversation.

- lack of cohesiveness within guidance staff
- too many tasks
- not enough training (computers, 504's)
- lack of communication w/ other school staff
- too many students to manage
- lack of supervision

2. The person doing the listening plays the critical role in this activity. The listener should spend a couple of minutes contemplating some feedback to his or her partner in response to the following questions:

   a. What three adjectives would you use to describe the person you just listened to?

   pessimistic, overwhelmed, downer

   b. If this person were your counselor, is there anything about him or her that you found distracting during this encounter? If so, what is it?

   not encouraging, negative, selfish

   c. If you were the superintendent of schools and you were interviewing this person for a counseling position in your district, what would you consider this person's assets as a candidate and what would you consider to be the deficits?

   Individual has clear understanding of system, analytical, can prioritize because they understand what is wrong w/ system

   d. As an extension of this activity, ask for responses to questions b and c from a family member or close friend.

Activity 2.3 Getting to Know Yourself

Take a personality assessment and ask for a thorough interpretive report. Think about how you would describe yourself to people who need to get to know you better. What can you tell them that can shed light on your uniqueness?

FUNCTIONING AS A TEAM

Peter Senge (1990) poses a poignant question in his book, *The Fifth Discipline: The Art & Practice of the Learning Organization,* by asking, "How can a team of committed leaders with individual IQs above 120 have a collective IQ of 63?" (p. 9). The problem with so many groups made up of highly intelligent and motivated individuals is that they spend inadequate time trying to understand and address the issues and agendas that are essential if the *group* is ever going to function as a *team.* This is too often the case for students in graduate school working together on projects, for steering committees working together to create new programs, for department chairs trying to agree on policy, for professional associations attempting to meet the needs of their constituents—and the list goes on and on. Senge explains that the discipline of team learning begins with dialogue, which depends on the capacity of members of a team to suspend assumptions and enter into genuine thinking together. It is no simple task; team development is a considerable challenge. The capacity of the group to move to a level of teamwork, however, is directly related to its ability to produce systemic changes that will have a major impact.

Cooperative Learning

Cooperative learning is an educational model that complements the team learning approach. Essentially, cooperative learning is one of the transferable skills that are taught in schools that have direct application to almost any group enterprise in the real world. Senge points out that learning teams need to find ways to practice together so that they can develop their collective learning skills. Omitting meaningful practice for collective learning is probably the predominant factor that keeps most management teams from being effective learning units. Cooperative learning in this book offers a means of practicing and rehearsing the skill needed to create better school counseling programs.

Cooperative learning embodies much of what the schools are about. In small groups, students apply their knowledge and understanding of task and maintenance issues of group process. They investigate topics through in-depth research, discussion, and debate; they use team problem-solving skills; they learn to analyze and synthesize information into a contextual framework that they all agree upon; and they use their creative energies to make presentations that educate, enlighten, and sometimes even entertain. Individuals who take full advantage of the cooperative learning experience find it to be empowering.

From a systemic perspective, cooperative learning activities should be a means of integrating several facets of a lesson, helping the participants to see the "big picture" and how the parts go together. Some of the further benefits of cooperative learning include:

1. Group members' strengths surface and are expressed.
2. Group pressure urges some members to new heights of performance, while other members learn how to encourage, motivate, and assert themselves.
3. Written and verbal communication are enhanced.
4. Team building and risk-taking can be fostered and nurtured.
5. Shared responsibility becomes an acceptable norm.
6. A more holistic perspective leads to results of higher quality.

Get ready to suspend your assumptions and enter into a process of learning and growth.

GROUP PROCESS SKILLS

We have seen too many examples where one dedicated individual would assume the responsibility for writing the school district's school counseling program plan and then everyone else would express their appreciation for the hard work, vote to accept the plan, and then relinquish any responsibility for carrying out the plan. We submit that having one person do the work may be quicker and easier, but it probably will not be better—and it certainly will not represent the collective thinking of important people who are affected by or responsible for the program. (Remember the definition of *accountability*?)

Sharing the leadership and the responsibility for developing and implementing a school counseling program takes longer and is a little harder to do. It is also more interesting and can be a lot more fun. The key to making this group experience a worthwhile venture, however, lies in everyone having a fundamental understanding of group process. We will provide you with a rather cursory overview of group process, recognizing that most counselors have had at least some course work in this area. We encourage you to find other sources of information that will assist you in getting all group members to contribute in meaningful ways to the group's task *and* process.

Activity 2.4   Setting the Stage

You will now begin the process of forming the groups (and ultimately the teams) that will provide the backdrop for learning and applying all the other skills that are introduced in this handbook.

1. If the learning is taking place in a college course, divide the class into groups of six or seven members. For school district counselors who are meeting to create a new counseling program plan, you have two choices: If you are from a small school district, continue to meet as one group if the size of the group does not exceed fifteen; if you are from a large school district, you will need to choose a planning team that carries out the tasks in this book, and then include the rest of the staff at different points in the process.

2. Make it a representative group. Each member of the group should assume the position of some member of the school or community. Some of the suggested positions are principal, counselor, media specialist, curriculum coordinator, classroom teacher, clerical staff, member of the business community, parent, and student. In the college classroom, this will be a role-playing situation; in schools, you may invite these representatives to be a part of your planning team. For classroom teams, we suggest you organize yourselves according to where people live, so that it is easier to communicate with one another outside of class.

3. After each group member has identified the position he or she is assuming, the group should spend some time discussing the various perspectives each of these individuals brings to the group. (A special note to counselor education students: although your major objective during this process is to learn the skills a counselor needs in order to create a school counseling program, you should regularly try to infuse some of the typical thinking and contributions that might be offered by the person whose job title you are representing on the work team, since this "mix of perspectives" will more closely resemble the realities you will ultimately face.)

4. Do not choose a leader yet, but just try to be conscious of what you are observing in the group and what your impressions are of various members of your group (focusing on positive thoughts, of course).

STAGES OF GROUP PROCESS

One of the most important lessons to learn about groups is that they move in and out of stages. Although many excellent theoretical models identify six or seven stages, we will use Tuckman's (1965) framework, since the terms used by Tuckman are so easy to remember. Tuckman referred to the four stages as *forming, storming, norming,* and *performing.*

The Forming Stage

This stage is often referred to as a time for getting acquainted. In the earliest phases of this stage, members recognize that they have gathered together for a common—but often nebulous—purpose. Activity 2.4, "Setting the Stage," was an example of this early stage of forming. Any group, throughout its life, will need to continue to "form" if it is expected to perform at higher levels; therefore, the forming stage is not an event that takes place before the other stages, but is a continuous process that lays the foundation for all other group work.

Several things need to be addressed in the forming stage:

- The membership of the group
- The purpose of the group
- Uncertainty about where members "fit"
- Attempts to understand the group—both its members and its issues
- Issues of trust
- Issues of cohesiveness
- The complexities of the group's dynamics

Activity 2.5   Forming Your Team

1. Your small group identified in the Activity 2.4 is now officially recognized as the steering committee for your school district. Your assignment is to develop a comprehensive developmental school counseling program *plan* that you will present to the school board at a future date.
2. For about twenty minutes, discuss the following:
   a. The implications of your group's responsibilities
   b. Questions that need answers
   c. Concerns about the task and process

Activity 2.6   Choosing Your Leaders

There are two major decisions your group must make that could have a significant impact on the final product you produce. You need to name a director of guidance and a scribe.

The choice of director of guidance makes a statement about the kind of leadership your group needs or by which it will allow itself to be influenced. For classroom cooperative learning groups, we usually encourage people to campaign for this position. A campaign allows people to assert themselves and highlights leadership skills. Often, groups take an extra week to decide on this important position because it gives people the chance to think about the significance of the choice, the potential for personal growth, and the decision of whether to campaign for the job. Every group member should be asking, "What kind of leader does this group need?" List some of your individual ideas here:

Ultimately, the group decides, and you need to make choices about whether the final decision is by majority rule, consensus, or default.

The scribe position is extremely important, as well. It has been said that the most powerful member of a committee is its secretary. What gets recorded and how it is recorded are fundamental to the final reports that surface from any group. A final product that is fraught with spelling and grammatical errors and omissions is a reflection on the group making the report. Therefore, your group's scribe should be able to convince you that her or his word processing skills are exemplary and that the final product of your group will make everyone proud.

Activity 2.7 Strengthening the Chain

An important adage that applies to teamwork is the one that states that a chain is only as strong as its weakest link. Everyone in a team needs to contribute talents and strengths to the completion of group tasks. Unfortunately, too often the less vocal or less assertive members of a group do not find opportunities to demonstrate their strengths and talents. During the forming stage, make a concerted effort to know and understand the other members of your team. Following are some possible *forming* exercises.

1. Have each person share five adjectives that are most descriptive of that person. Brief explanations may help. What are your five adjectives?

2. Have each person explain some contributions he or she has made to previous groups.
3. Have group members express their aspirations for the group.
4. If people have taken a personality assessment, have them explain their results.
5. Have group members talk about any bad experiences they have had in groups in the past. What did they learn from those experiences?
6. Have group members explain to everyone the kind of group member they hope to be in this group.

The Storming Stage

In this second stage, group members need to appreciate the fact that the group *should* be experiencing some frustration, confusion, and disorientation as the group's goals are more clearly defined. The storming stage is not always stormy, but it can be unsettling. Since the group is still in the process of forming, participants are seeking purpose, clarity of mission, direction, and security in the group. Often, members will consciously or unconsciously assert the roles they hope to play within the group. This is also a time when group members are trying to decide whether they want to be or will be committed to the group's mission.

There are three complementary and essential aspects of the group process that deserve considerable attention during this storming stage: risk-taking, trust-building, and communication. Risk-taking is essential for helping group members both to share their concerns and vulnerabilities in the group and to be more creative and innovative in developing the program. Risk-taking, however, can happen only in an environment of trust, so the group will have to rely on some thoughtful norms in the next stage to nurture that trust. A fundamental goal during the storming stage should be to *promote understanding;* therefore, the more group members practice good communication skills—especially listening, the more they will be able to understand each other and the group's mission. Good communication skills can help build trust in the group's process.

Group leaders will need to use their best facilitation skills to promote *good* storming that helps to "clear the air" and to build the kind of cohesive group that can produce at high levels. The storming stage is usually the most important stage, and if a team learns to move through this stage patiently and thoughtfully, the members of the team will have learned one of the most important lessons of functioning as a team.

Activity 2.8   The Trust Factor

1. Think about some of your past group experiences in which the lack of a trusting environment contributed to group problems. What were some of the factors or situations that diminished the levels of trust in these groups? Share these factors with your group.

- not committed to project
- lack of participation
- lack of confidence
- rude to group members
- lack of communication

2. What factors must exist in your steering committee for you to "trust the process"?

- guidance
- expectations / boundaries set
- participation
-

The Norming Stage

Norms are essentially the rules by which a group operates. The classic example of norming is when organizations agree to operate according to parliamentary procedure. Now, we are not suggesting that your steering committee conduct its business according to rigid rules and regulations, but we do want to encourage you to consciously outline some of the expected behaviors and procedures that will guide your work.

Groups often have *implicit* norms that are more powerful than their *explicit* norms. For example, if group members regularly show up ten to fifteen minutes late to committee meetings and the meetings do not begin until everyone is there, it becomes clear before too long that the implicit rule is that meetings do not start on time. Good group members become conscious of these implicit norms and bring them to the attention of the group if they appear to be undermining the effectiveness of the group. The group can then decide whether explicit norms are needed to help the group stay focused.

Activity 2.9   Setting Norms

1. Individually, list five or six norms that you believe are essential if the group is to function well as a team.

- trust
- communication
- mutual respect
- start w/ end in sight
- completion of work
- openness
- value differences
- confidentiality

2. Share the individual lists in the steering committee group. Come to a consensus (a normative procedure) on five or six norms that will set the tone for your group's work. See this list as a working draft—that is, come back to the list after the group has met several times and decide whether the list should be altered to more accurately meet the group's needs. The norming stage starts evolving as leadership begins to emerge.

Activity 2.10   Brainstorming

Since we suggest several activities throughout the book that involve brainstorming, we will list the basic rules of brainstorming here for your reference. Setting norms for some of the procedures we use, such as brainstorming, can, in turn, make the *storming* process more understandable and effective. Carefully observe these brainstorming rules as you seek input from your groups, since this activity is often a key focus for planning and creating new programs and initiatives:

1. One or two people should take responsibility for writing everything down, preferably on a chalkboard or on newsprint.
2. Any idea, no matter how unusual, should be shared and recorded.
3. Build on each other's ideas.
4. Every idea is as good as every other idea—putdowns are not allowed.
5. Do not analyze or critique any suggestions during brainstorming; save that until all ideas have been recorded. As a steering committee, discuss the challenges associated with the use of brainstorming techniques in work groups.

The Performing Stage

This stage is also referred to as the working stage. Because group members understand each other and the parameters of their assignments, have operated according to the group's norms, and trust the power of the group's process, they will often volunteer for tasks in which their strengths will surface, and they will become invested in the group's accomplishments.

The performing stage *happens* if the group has given sufficient attention to the complexities of the previous stages. Once the groups have reached the performing stage, however, they can also expect to revisit earlier stages on a regular basis. In fact, a group is always in the stage of forming, since each new encounter provides a different opportunity to learn something new about group members and the dynamics of the group as a whole.

Although this model of group process is presented as a sequential stage model, it is obvious that groups, because of their dynamic nature, might be actively engaged in two or three stages *at the same time!* For example, group members can discover interesting insights about each other (forming) as they debate (storm) and agree upon the norms by which they will function. Experience tells us that creating a comprehensive developmental school counseling program plan will move a group through two or more stages every time you meet, and that is why it is necessary for group members to continuously assess how their cooperative learning is doing.

TASK AND MAINTENANCE ISSUES

Groups that effectively progress through the stages of group process must strike a balance between attending to the tasks the group must accomplish and the interpersonal dynamics of the group. Pfeiffer and Jones (1976) have outlined some of the various roles that group members play in contributing to the balance—or inbalance—between these task and maintenance issues. Figure 2.1 provides a list of some typical roles that can be observed in working groups. Note, though, that Pfeiffer and Jones refer to this list as a *partial* list of possible roles. Good group facilitators and informed group members need to understand the various contributions or dysfunctional roles that are contributing to the dynamics of a group if they are going to be empowered to influence the group's effectiveness.

The members of an efficient and productive group must provide for meeting two kinds of needs—what it takes to do the job, and what it takes to strengthen and maintain the group. What members do to serve group needs may be called functional roles. Statements and behaviors that tend to make the group inefficient or weak may be called nonfunctional behaviors.

Role Functions in a Group

A. **Task Roles** (functions required in selecting and carrying out a group task)
   1. *Initiating Activity:* Proposing solutions, suggesting new ideas, new definitions of the problem, new attack on the problem, or new organization of material.
   2. *Seeking Information:* Asking for clarification of suggestions, requesting additional information or facts.
   3. *Seeking Opinion:* Looking for an expression of feeling about something from the members, seeking clarification of values, suggestions, or ideas.
   4. *Giving Information:* Offering facts or generalizations, relating one's experience to the group problem to illustrate points.,
   5. *Giving Opinion:* Stating an opinion or belief concerning a suggestion or one of several suggestions, particularly concerning its value rather than its factual basis.
   6. *Elaborating:* Clarifying, giving examples or developing meanings, trying to envision how a proposal might work if adopted.
   7. *Coordinating:* Showing relationships among various ideas or suggestions, trying to pull ideas and suggestions together.
   8. *Summarizing:* Pulling together related suggestions or ideas, restating suggestions after the group has discussed them.

B. **Group Building and Maintenance Roles** (functions required in strengthening and maintaining group life and activities)
   1. *Encouraging:* Being friendly, warm, responsive to others, praising others and their ideas, agreeing with and accepting contributions of others.
   2. *Gatekeeping:* Trying to make it possible for another to make a contribution to the group by saying, "We haven't heard from Jim yet," or suggesting limited talking time for everyone so that all will have a chance to be heard.
   3. *Standard Setting:* Expressing standards for the group to use in choosing its content or procedures or in evaluating its decisions, reminding group to avoid decisions that conflict with group standards.
   4. *Following:* Going along with decisions of the group, thoughtfully accepting ideas of others, serving as audience during group discussion.
   5. *Expressing Group Feeling:* Summarizing what group feeling is sensed to be, describing reactions of the group to ideas or solutions.

C. **Both Group Task and Maintenance Roles**
   1. *Evaluating:* Submitting group decisions or accomplishments to comparison with group standards, measuring accomplishments against goals.
   2. *Diagnosing:* Determining sources of difficulties, appropriate steps to take next, analyzing the main blocks to progress.
   3. *Testing for Consensus:* Tentatively asking for group opinions in order to find out whether the group is reaching consensus on a decision, sending up trial balloons to test group opinions.

Figure 2.1

Reprinted from J. William Pfeiffer and John E. Jones (Eds.), 1976, *The 1976 Handbook for Group Facilitators*, San Diego, CA: University Associates.

  4. *Mediating:* Harmonizing, conciliating differences in points of view, making compromise solutions.

  5. *Relieving tension:* Draining off negative feeling by jesting or pouring oil on troubled waters, putting a tense situation in wider context.

D. **Types of Nonfunctional Behavior**

  1. *Being Aggressive:* Working for status by criticizing or blaming others, showing hostility against the group or some individual, deflating the ego or status of others.

  2. *Blocking:* Interfering with the progress of the group by going off on a tangent, citing personal experiences unrelated to the problem, arguing too much on a point, rejecting ideas without consideration.

  3. *Self-Confession:* Using the group as a sounding board, expressing personal, nongroup-oriented feelings or points of view.

  4. *Competing:* Vying with others to produce the best idea, talk the most, play the most roles, gain favor with the leader.

Figure 2.1 Continued

  A partial list of the kinds of contributions or the group services that are performed by one or many individuals is shown in Figure 2.1. In using this or any other classification, people need to guard against the tendency to blame any person (whether themselves or another) whose actions fall into a "nonfunctional behavior" category. It is more useful to regard such behavior as a symptom that all is not well with the group's ability to satisfy individual needs through group-centered activity. People need to be alert to the fact that each person is likely to interpret such behaviors differently. What appears to be nonfunctional behavior may not be necessarily so, for the content and the group conditions also must be taken into account.

Activity 2.11 Understanding Roles

  1. Individually, using Figure 2.1 as a resource, list the two or three major roles that you typically play in groups.

  2. Share your identified roles with your steering committee group. Invite feedback about whether they have observed you in these roles. Have they seen you playing other prominent roles?

  3. Explore other roles that did not make the Pfeiffer and Jones list that you have witnessed in groups. Can these additional roles fit under the task, maintenance, or nonfunctional behavior role categories?

4. As your steering committee continues to work together, it will need to assess whether the important roles are being assumed by group members and/or whether certain roles need more attention if the group is to evolve as a working and learning team.

SYNERGY IN GROUPS

Good teams continually build on the strengths of their members. As Senge (1990) pointed out, individual power can only contribute to synergy when the various powers of a learning team are aligned. Synergy is typically described as a condition in which the whole is greater than the sum of its parts. Covey (1989) also suggested that synergy means that "the relationship which the parts have to each other is a part in and of itself. It is not only a part, but the most catalytic, the most empowering, the most unifying, and the most exciting part" (p. 263).

It is our hope that this book will provide a framework and the tools for helping school counselors work toward synergistic school counseling programs. We recognize, however, that the essential component of such synergistic programs evolves from the members of the teams that create the programs—that is, from the human factor. Myriad tasks can be accomplished and deadlines can be met, but without proper attention to team building, synergy cannot be achieved.

We encourage you to come back to some of the group process activities in this chapter from time to time. Your careful attention to some of the group process at work in your group is a critical feature of this book. If you learn some of the substantive lessons of group process by working on this cooperative learning team, you will gain an extremely significant skill for working with a team of school counselors and coworkers to create high-quality school counseling programs. As a current or future change agent in the schools, you will also be learning skills that will assist your schools in such efforts as school restructuring and site-based management.

Activity 2.12   The Process Observer

This final activity integrates many of the lessons from this chapter and introduces a very powerful resource for helping groups attend to their group process needs. A group process observer is usually a person who does not participate in the business (task) issues of the group, but instead puts his or her energy into the objective observation of the group's "process." Groups that are interested in receiving feedback about their team's effectiveness should consider using a process observer. Often, groups will bring someone in from outside who has some expertise in group work and who is not invested in the responsibilities and dynamics of the group to be observed. However, this is not always possible for a variety of reasons. Therefore, we offer the Group Process Observer Guide in Figure 2.2 as a framework that can be used for conducting a group process observation. *At least twice during the time your steering committee is working together, have someone who has completed at least one course in group process and procedures act as the process observer, using the guide in Figure 2.2 to outline feedback for your group.*

Summary

In this chapter, we have given you a framework and some of the tools to form working teams or groups in order to accomplish the task of creating and implementing a comprehensive developmental school counseling program. As you work through the remaining chapters and add other tools, be sure to complete the reflection questions at the end of each chapter.

Group Process Observer Guide

I. GROUP INFORMATION:

    A. Name of group: _____

    B. Nature/type of group: _____

    C. Number in group: _____

    D. Is there a designated leader? _____ Yes _____ No

    E. Are there assigned roles? _____ Yes _____ No

    F. How long has the group been together? _____

    G. Other:

II. OBSERVATIONS:

    1. Describe the behavior of the group:

    2. What leadership behaviors are being demonstrated?

    3. Are the group's goals clear? _____ Yes _____ No What do they appear to be?

    4. What are the various roles being played by group members?

    5. Does the group operate by explicit or implicit norms or both? _____ What are they?

Figure 2.2

6. How cohesive is the group?

   What are the indicators of cohesion (or lack of cohesion)?

7. Does the group attend more to task issues or maintenance issues? _____
   Is the balance appropriate for the group's goals? _____ Yes _____ No
   Other comments about the task/maintenance balance:

8. Describe the interpersonal dynamics of this group (including patterns of communication):

9. Do there appear to be hidden agendas that affect the dynamics of the group?
   _____ Yes _____ No   If yes, what do they seem to be?

10. Other observations:

III. QUESTIONS THAT HAVE SURFACED AS A RESPONSE TO THE GROUP OBSERVATION:

   1.

   2.

   3.

   4.

   5.

Figure 2.2 Continued

IV. MAJOR AREAS OF CONCERN/HYPOTHESES/HIGHLIGHTS:

V. RECOMMENDATIONS:

Observer: _____   Date: _____

Figure 2.2 Continued

Completing these reflections will help you obtain your final product more effectively as well as keep track of your work in progress.

References

Cattell, R. B., & IPAT Staff. (1991). *16 PF© Sixteen Personality Factor Questionnaire*. Champaign, IL: The Institute for Personality and Ability Testing, Inc.

Covey, S. R. (1989). *The 7 habits of highly successful people*. New York: Simon & Schuster.

Myers, I. B., & Briggs, K. (1992). *Myers-Briggs Type Indicator*. Palo Alto, CA: Counseling Psychologists Press.

Pfeiffer, J. W., & Jones, J. E. (Eds.). (1976). *The 1976 handbook for group facilitators*. San Diego, CA: Pfeiffer & Company.

Senge, P. (1990). *The fifth discipline: The art & practice of the learning organization*. New York: Currency/Doubleday.

Tuckman, B. (1965). Developmental sequence in small groups. *Psychological Bulletin, 63*, 384–399.

Reflections on Chapter 2

1. Explain why it is important to emphasize the human factor.

2. What is some of the work your group still needs to do to become a team?

3. At this time, what do you see as your contribution to your team?

4. Describe some of the frustrations that you felt as you worked with the activities in this chapter.

5. What questions do you have for yourself, your group members, or your facilitator?

6. Notes:

Chapter 3

Conceptualizing the Program

Counselors need to experience and appreciate the development of a comprehensive school counseling program from the beginning to the final product. Through such involvement, you will be able to see why certain projects and activities evolve as priorities and why others receive little or no attention. Before you can start narrowing your options, however, you must first ponder all your possibilities. This chapter provides an opportunity for you to imagine and anticipate the wide range of actions that contribute to the development and success of a total program. We will provide you with learning activities, such as brainstorming and flowcharting skills, that will help you conceptualize the program—from the beginning to the final product.

SEEING THE BIG PICTURE

In Chapter 1, we introduced you to Covey's model of interdependence and Senge's disciplines of a learning organization. Both authors emphasize the importance of seeing the big picture. Seeing the big picture means having a broad view of the total undertaking, and it is fundamental to creating and maintaining a program that is truly comprehensive and developmental. Seeing this way involves higher-level thinking, comprehension, and the ability to synthesize. Counselors with this kind of vision can take an ill-defined conglomeration of tasks and activities, and mold them into a well-integrated program.

Seeing the big picture is another way of talking about *systemic thinking*. In this handbook, we will not probe deeply into systems analysis, but we will introduce you to some basic concepts that will help lay the foundation for sound program management practices. A good place to begin is with some definitions. Essentially, *a system* is a structure whose orderly whole is comprised of integral parts (subsystems) that function together to accomplish a specific mission. *Systemic thinking, then, is both seeking to understand goals and tasks within the context of the system's mission—and acting in purposeful ways to contribute to that mission.*

Activity 3.1   Making Sense of Systems

In your groups, investigate *each* concept in the definitions given above. Keeping in mind the enormous task of developing a K–12 comprehensive developmental school counseling program, discuss the implications of the following questions:

1. What do we mean by *structure*?
2. What is an *orderly whole*?

3. What are integral parts or *subsystems*?
4. What is the significance of the term *function together*?
5. How does the term *accomplish* fit into the definition of a system?
6. What do we mean by *mission*?

After discussing these concepts, have at least one member of the group describe a system in lay terms.

One of the outstanding characteristics of a system is that it fosters "intentional achievement." If your goal is to achieve an excellent school counseling program, then it is imperative for you to create a process that enables you to reach that goal in the most efficient and responsible manner. We are going to demonstrate one way of intentionally envisioning the integral parts functioning together to create a systemic whole.

DEVELOPING A FLOWCHART

One of the more useful tools for conceptualizing a system is the *flowchart*. Even though many flowcharts are as complex as the circuit board of a major electronic device, we nonetheless have grown to appreciate them for the way they help us see the big picture. One of the most beneficial aspects of developing and using a flowchart is that everyone involved in a project has the same visual picture of the system in which they are working.

Flowcharts created by big businesses are often complex and filled with technical jargon, but they can be much simpler. Here we are giving you a slimmed-down, user-friendly version that employs a limited number of guidelines.

Most of you have had to create an outline at various times in your life. (You know the rules: each major heading starts with a Roman numeral, the subcategories under those headings begin with a capital letter, you must have at least two entries in each category, and so on.) Flowcharting is very much like creating an outline. The nice thing about the flowchart is that it usually can be displayed on a single piece of paper.

There are key terms to remember in creating a flowchart:

1. Function box
2. Descriptors
3. Function codes
4. Signal paths
5. Cumulation dots
6. Feedback loops
7. Feed forward loops (We know, it sounds like your VCR!)

Follow along as we explain these terms.

Function Box

Each major part or function of any system is entitled to a prominent place in the flowchart that highlights its significance (similar to those elements that are worthy of a Roman numeral in an outline). To illustrate with a simple example, if your goal is to present a seminar or presentation, there are typically four major functions to consider. These are illustrated in the *function boxes* in Figure 3.1.

As the flowchart becomes more sophisticated, we need to include *subfunctions* in each of the function boxes. For example, under the Planning function, there may be subfunctions such as Determine Need, Identify Audience, Select Site, Select Time, and so on. The subfunctions in a flowchart are the "integral parts" that were highlighted in the definition of a system.

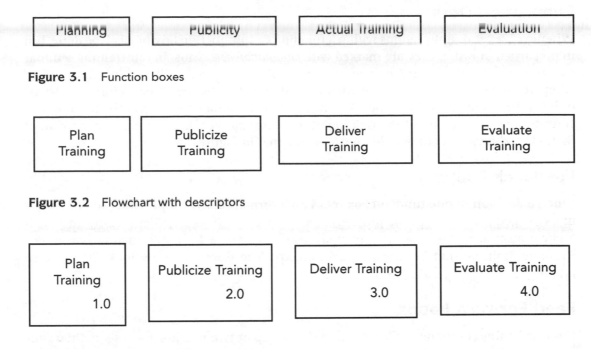

| Planning | Publicity | Actual Training | Evaluation |

Figure 3.1 Function boxes

| Plan Training | Publicize Training | Deliver Training | Evaluate Training |

Figure 3.2 Flowchart with descriptors

| Plan Training 1.0 | Publicize Training 2.0 | Deliver Training 3.0 | Evaluate Training 4.0 |

Figure 3.3 Flowchart with function codes

Activity 3.2   Subfunctions

Take a few moments to list some of the subfunctions on chart paper that would be listed in each of the function boxes in Figure 3.1. Use the following headings.

Planning	**Publicity**	**Actual Training**	**Evaluation**
Choose date / time Identify speakers	• Contact public- ations • Create invitations	Set-up site Distribute packets	Survey participants Collect data

Descriptors

So that everyone uses a common style of language, we suggest that you use *action verbs* to describe each function. Also, you need to state the function as clearly and concisely as possible so that everyone using the flowchart has the common understanding required for intentional achievement to take place. Try to limit *descriptors* to five words or fewer. Thus, the flowchart takes on a slightly new appearance (see Figure 3.2).

Function Codes

Most projects have a sequential order; one thing must be done before the next thing can be accomplished. In Figures 3.1 and 3.2, the functions have an obvious sequence. To denote the order of events, we assign *function codes*, which provide a numerical sequence (Figure 3.3). Thus, our flowchart takes on the look shown in Figure 3.3.

Signal Paths

To find your way on any map, you need to have a sense of direction or some clear signals that direct your way. *Signal paths* are arrows that show the exact route to take in progressing through the flowchart. A new dimension is added in Figure 3.4 to illustrate the *signal paths*.

Cumulation Dots

Whenever several subfunctions within a function or subfunction box must all be done, but in no particular order, they are marked with *cumulation dots*. Thus, in our training seminar example, the fourth *sub-subfunction box* under "Plan Training" will identify the need to "Prepare Materials." Several different materials need to be prepared before the actual training, but in no particular order. As long as all the materials show up at the training and contribute to the quality of the training, it does not matter which ones get taken care of first. The subfunction box would now look like that in Figure 3.5.

Feedback Loops

When a decision in one function box relies on information from a previous box or results in a changed procedure in the previous box, we use a *feedback loop*, denoted by an *F* with a circle around it. For example, we may want to have a fifth subfunction box under Evaluate Training that becomes a Decision Box. The flowchart now looks like that in Figure 3.6.

Feed Forward Loops

Essentially, this component allows you to skip a step or two in a normally sequential routine. In our example, during the Planning phase, one of the subfunctions may be to choose a training site. Some training sites require formal contracts, so we may want to

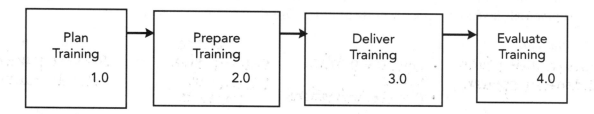

Figure 3.4 Flowchart with signal paths

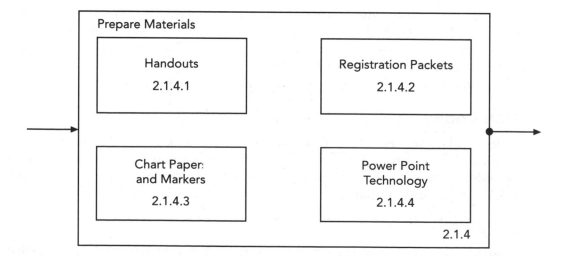

Figure 3.5 Flowchart with cumulation dots

anticipate that step; however, the feed forward loop illustrates how we can skip a step if it is not needed. The feed forward loop is denoted by *FF*, with a circle around the letters. Figure 3.7 shows how the feed forward loop works.

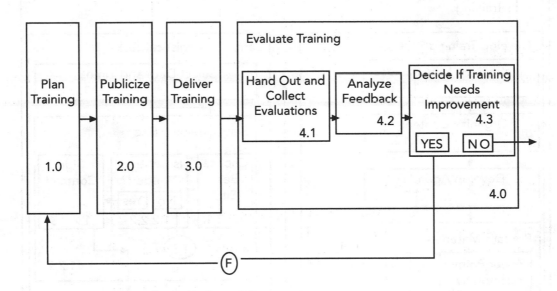

Figure 3.6 Flowchart with feedback loops

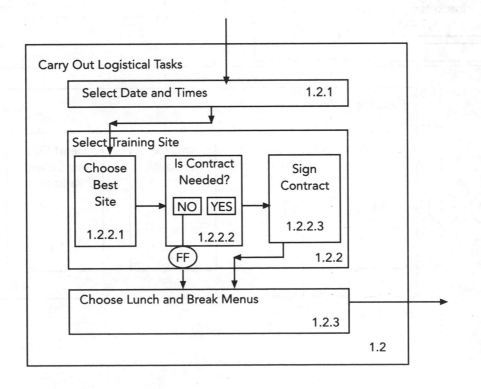

Figure 3.7 Flowchart with feed forward loops

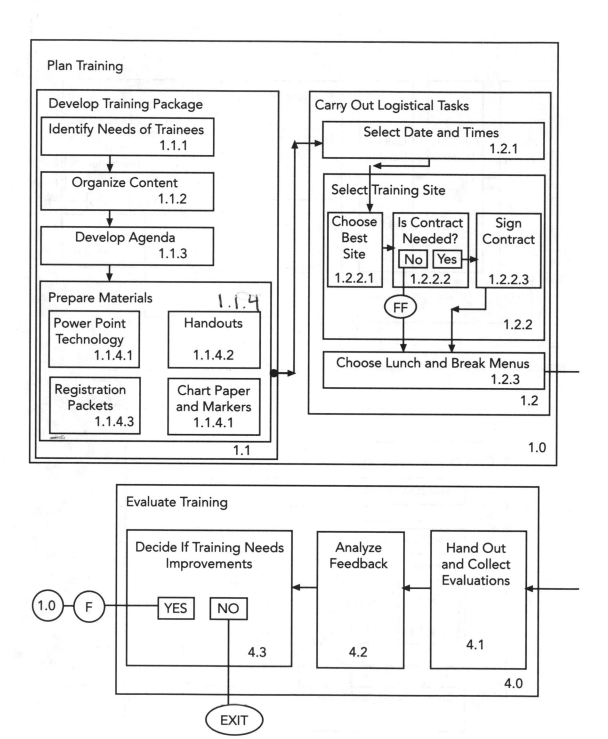

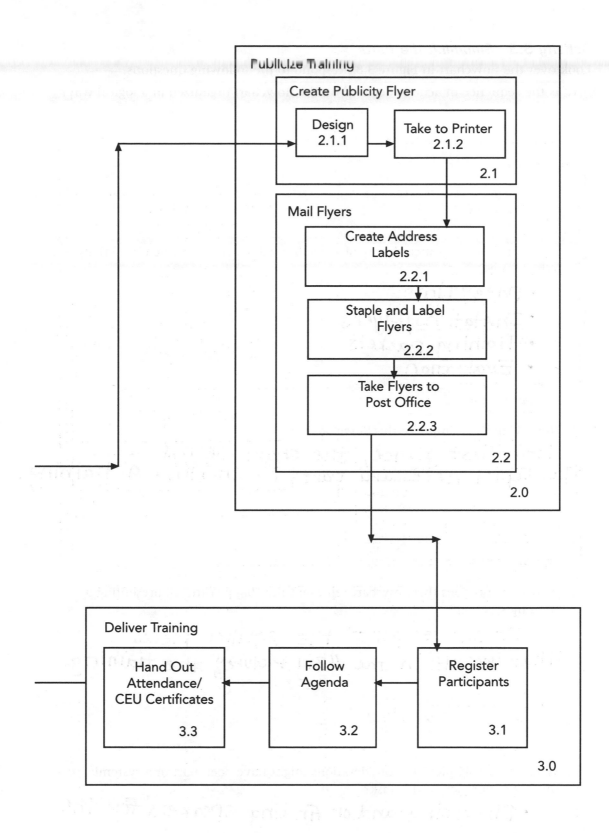

Figure 3.8 Systemic training

Activity 3.3 Summing the Parts

Look over the flowchart in Figure 3.8. Respond to the following questions.

1. Is the sequence of actions depicted on the flowchart organized in a logical way?

2. Does this flowchart include any of the subfunctions you identified in Activity 3.2? Which ones?

- Date / Time
- Invitations / Flyers
- Training packets
- Evaluation

3. How would you improve this flowchart?

From first glance, the chart seems to depict necessary parts of creating a training.

4. In what ways does this flowchart represent the "big picture" of presenting a training seminar?

It shows all of the smaller pieces that result in the "Big Picture", the training.

5. What other "big picture" considerations might have been part of a systemic thinker's approach to this task?

- Discussing and or finding speakers for the event.
- creating committees

THE TOTAL PICTURE

Note that in looking at all the steps, we have discovered that the task of conducting a training seminar is not just a simple four-step process, but that it can be expanded to include a number of functions and subfunctions that are fairly distinct and yet really quite complex. The flowchart in Figure 3.8 shows the combined parts working together to make a more complete whole.

Later, when you explore some of the major functions of a comprehensive developmental school counseling program, we hope you will *not* spend time on minutiae like "Fill the coffee pot," but will focus on the primary actions that need to be taken to accomplish your goal. We have led you through this rather detailed lesson to demonstrate the importance of how things function together to make a whole. The skills of analyzing and synthesizing, if learned well, can empower you for the rest of your life as they help you envision the entire program and all its parts.

Activity 3.4 Developing a Flowchart: Trial Run

In small groups, choose one of the following three projects:

1. Plan an end-of-semester party. (theme based)
2. Plan how you will write a term paper.
3. Plan a trip.

Design a flowchart to illustrate the sequence of your plan. It should take twenty to thirty minutes to generate a "rough" flowchart that generally depicts your group's version of the big picture and its parts.

Describe your flowchart to the rest of the class. Also, describe the process your group used to plan.

Discuss what you have learned about systems thinking. List some of the highlights here:

If you have done a really good job, why not carry out your plan (especially if your group chose option 1)?

Activity 3.5 Developing a Flowchart Prototype

You are now going to begin work on a flowchart for developing a comprehensive school counseling program that represents the thinking of your small group. Without looking ahead to future chapters, use the blank flowchart in Figure 3.9 and the list of major functions that appears in the following text to create a sequence of functions that might represent a tentative district plan for a comprehensive developmental school counseling program. This flowchart will become your working model. You will probably change it somewhat as you gain new knowledge of the functions and activities needed for planning and implementing a comprehensive school counseling program. Your task in this activity, however, is to begin the "sorting out" stage of conceptualizing the big picture.

Figure 3.9 Blank flowchart for planning a comprehensive school counseling program. Identify major functions, assign subfunctions, and draw in signal paths.

You do not have to use all the boxes, or you may choose to add more or enlarge some. Your task as a group is to use the major functions *to create a flowchart that you believe will determine the sequence that will move your group toward the development of a comprehensive school counseling program.*

Major Functions (in alphabetical order)

1. Assign responsibilities
2. Conceptualize the program
3. Conduct program research and evaluation
4. Create guidance program
5. Determine program priorities
6. Develop public awareness and support

7. Examine program models
8. Organize program support
9. Promote professional development

10. Provide leadership and supervision
11. Refine the model

You have (tentatively) created the basic flowchart that you will use throughout this course. Congratulations on becoming a systems thinker! Now, try assigning some of the subfunctions in their appropriate boxes.

Subfunctions (in random order)

Select advisory committee
Prepare budget
Develop counselor evaluation
Disseminate results
Review established models
Adopt evaluation plan
Explore grant writing
Address the human factor
Identify individual leadership strengths
Identify program coordinator
Identify resources
Plan inservice education

Plan for peer supervision
Complete professional development plans
Identify professional growth opportunities
Establish program/clinical supervision
Explore program considerations
Design program evaluation
Develop public relations plan
Publish articles
Identify research projects
Create skill-building activities
Suggest changes in program

We want to emphasize that this is just a *sample* of the many subfunctions that could be included in a systemic plan for a school counseling program.

Activity 3.6   Plan the Plan

Now that you have the big picture in mind, you have a sense of the task before you. In the weeks ahead, your group needs to generate the substantive content that will build on the foundation provided by the flowchart and demonstrate in what ways your plan is truly *comprehensive* and *developmental*.

1. Your group's task at this point is to return once again to brainstorming. Spend about ten minutes naming as many things as you can think of that must be accomplished before your group ultimately makes a presentation to the other groups in class that will be acting as your school board. At the presentation, you will unveil your comprehensive developmental school counseling program plan. (If you are practicing school counselors using the model to redesign your program, at this point you need to identify the group to which you will initially present your plan.)

2. Take your ideas from the brainstorming session and use them to develop a new flowchart, illustrating how your group will function in the weeks ahead. It is usually a good idea to determine what you want your final product or task to be and then work backward to determine what you must do first. Everything in between the first step and the final product needs to be sequenced to take you step by step to the successful fulfillment of your plan. Be as detailed as you need to be. Keep in mind that both task and maintenance roles, as explained in Chapter 2 (Figure 2.1), may need attention as you proceed in this group effort.

Activity 3.7 Assuming and Assigning Responsibility

As an extension of Activity 3.6, "Plan the Plan," you may want to assign members of your group to assume responsibility for various tasks that have been identified through your brainstorming and refinement efforts. Sharing the load is important. You will need ample opportunity for group members to share their accomplishments and to ask questions that will assure everyone that you are all headed in the same direction. The following list will get you started, and you can add to the list as the tasks become apparent:

Major Tasks

Facilitator of Group

Compiling/Synthesizing Written Work

Gatekeeper

Art Work

Chart Maker

Data Collector

Person Responsible

Director of Guidance:

Scribe:

A SUGGESTED FORMAT FOR YOUR PLAN OF ACTION

As you begin to develop a plan of action, consider the following:

1. Where will you meet as a group? Choose a setting that is comfortable but helps the group stay focused, cooperative, and productive.
2. When will you begin? The obvious answer is right now. Do not wait for others or other groups to begin. Instead, set the pace for others to follow.
3. When do you want to finish? This step and the previous one determine the time frame in which your group must accomplish its tasks.
4. How will you begin? What steps will come next, and what steps will follow those? Apply the concepts presented in this and subsequent chapters to your own planning. Use *action verbs* in identifying how you will get things done.
5. In what sequence do you need to proceed? You have a working flowchart to guide you in this process. Remember that it is only a guide. *Revisit your flowchart and this chapter frequently.* Doing so will keep you on your task.
6. Who does what? Make maximum use of the strengths of all members of your planning group. Who else needs to be involved in the planning process?

We want to point out that in the past thirty years, the combined number of "formal" flowcharts prepared by the two of us does not exceed ten. In no way does that number suggest that flowcharts are unimportant or insignificant in what we do. What it does suggest is that we reserve the process of flowcharting for *very* important missions—those that deserve a great deal of vision, collective energy, and strategic planning. Creating a comprehensive developmental school counseling program definitely belongs in the category of very important missions. It is the most important task you can address as a professional school counselor. Systemic thinking may not always be fun, but it is one of the most critical competencies you can develop if you want your program to succeed. If you are able to appreciate—not necessarily enjoy—the depth of thinking that goes into formal flowcharting, then you are on the right path to becoming at least an "informal" systemic thinker, which is the kind of thinking you will use most often, anyway.

Summary

This chapter has discussed some of the fundamental skills you will need to adequately plan and ultimately implement a school counseling program that is holistic, sequential, focused, integrated, and accountable. You may need to spend more than one week exploring the activities in this chapter, and you may need to return to them to refocus your group's efforts. Discover where the feedback loops are needed, and return to this chapter to get back on track—as any good systems thinker would do.

Reflections on Chapter 3

1. Describe the benefits of flowcharting.

   Organizes info in a logical format

2. What do you find frustrating about flowcharting?

   The boxes, arrows, dots & circles...
   it can be difficult to determine which to use.

3. Where else in your life will flowcharting help you?

   Organizing semester work + projects

4. How has this chapter helped you to see the big picture?

   It taught me to focus on one small piece at
   a time because eventually all the pieces will
   come together to form the "big picture!"

5. What questions do you have for yourself, your group members, or your facilitator?

6. Notes:

 ## Chapter 4

Examining
Program Models

Few topics are as important to school counselors as how to organize their
[counseling] programs. . . . When school guidance and counseling is organized
to meet specific goals and objectives and careful attention is directed towards
"who will accomplish what," the evidence suggests that both the deliverers
(counselors and school faculty) and students and parents are more satisfied.

—Gysbers & Henderson, 1994

For decades, a majority of counselor education programs trained counselors to use a therapeutic model within the public elementary and secondary schools. Counselors in training learned, and learned well, to counsel students one-on-one. Often, they would then locate within a school system where they were expected to "hit the ground running," and they delivered the guidance activities that were expected of them by their principal and/or board of education.

The counselors who located in large schools might have been hired to be the "adjustment" counselors and, indeed, might have been able to work with individual clients. Those located in medium-sized schools were probably expected to provide a number of different services, including college counseling, career counseling, referral, and follow-up. More often than not, these new graduates found themselves in a one-counselor school where they were expected to carry out all the services and programs usually conducted by an experienced director. These new counselors might have had a course in organization and administration of counseling programs, but it was probably not a major emphasis in a total program that emphasized therapeutic counseling.

In the 1970s and 1980s, many counselor education programs began to move from a therapeutic, or medical, model that is designed to deliver services to specific populations to a comprehensive or developmental model that is designed to deliver programs to all the students within the school. The need for an appropriate organizational structure that provides counseling programs to all students was finally being addressed.

In 1978, Gysbers described a program model that was the foundation for this new emphasis on counseling programs integrated into the total educational program of the school district. This emphasis defines the competencies that students develop through participation in a comprehensive school counseling program. These competencies drive the total program and are carried with the students as they become adults. The competencies can be achieved in a number of ways programmatically.

We will not detail all the possible models for developing comprehensive school counseling programs, but there are many excellent texts that provide informative and structured frameworks for understanding the complexities of such programs. These texts are highly respected by counselor educators and practitioners. (See the list at the end of this chapter, which includes a representative sample of textbooks used in the United States.) Our expectation is that by the time you have completed the procedures and activities in this handbook, you will have developed a program that incorporates the major components of the text you are using into a working model of excellence. It is important to have, and perhaps to display where all can see, a model that becomes the center of attention in your program. We will explain several models that are being successfully used in most parts of the United States. These models are patterned after other existing models, especially the Missouri (Gysbers) model; and they have been developed and are being implemented by local, regional, and state practitioners. Your challenge will be to glean from these models the appropriate structures that will make it possible for you to conceptualize your own program.

THE MISSOURI MODEL

Briefly stated, the Missouri model organizes the program into four major components: guidance curriculum, individual planning, responsive services, and system support (sometimes referred to as program management). Too many school counseling programs spend inordinate amounts of time in one arena, while providing few services in other areas. There are enough issues that need attention in schools so that counselors could have more than enough to do by just focusing on "putting out fires." Such a mode of operation, however, is based on a reactive, not a proactive, model. A developmental model, on the other hand, tries to reduce reactive services and put most of the energy into prevention through a well-balanced program model.

The New Hampshire adaptation of the Missouri model depicted in Figure 4.1 shows how one state used the four major components, as well as adding other dimensions that reflect the ASCA National Standards for School Counseling Programs. Those who developed the New Hampshire model added a "life roles" component; the person in the center of the diagram demonstrates that people are the most important part of the program.

In the next section, we will briefly describe each component of the Missouri model and give you an activity that fits within that component. We recommend that each work group develop one of the next three activities, report out their findings to the whole class, and receive suggestions from the others.

The Guidance Curriculum

Although all aspects of a comprehensive developmental school guidance and counseling program are important, the guidance curriculum is at the very heart of the program. Without it, counselors are seen as merely providing a variety of services with no particular focus. The guidance curriculum is the vehicle for *delivering* a program that is truly comprehensive and developmental. The guidance curriculum is an integral part of the total school's curriculum; it is not an add-on. School counselors should be creative in integrating the guidance curriculum with subject-area curricula so that students can see the interrelationships in their learning and the practical applications of the guidance curriculum.

New Hampshire Comprehensive Guidance and Counseling Program

A Guide to an Approved Model for Program Development

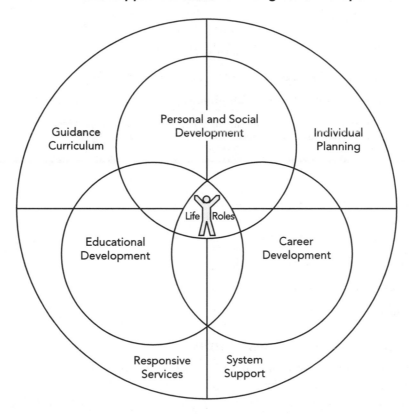

Figure 4.1 Adaptation of the Missouri model as used in the New Hampshire model

Activity 4.1 Identifying Learning Outcomes

To get you started thinking in creative ways about how to integrate curriculum, we provide two examples of learning outcomes. Identify which of the activities aimed at these learning outcomes can be (1) taught by a classroom teacher as part of a course, (2) learned within a family or community setting separate from the school, or (3) team taught by a counselor and a teacher within a classroom or small group. Discuss the role of the counselor in each situation. Also, identify the earliest grade in a K–12 system in which the learning outcome could (or should) be addressed. Figure 4.2 contains the learning outcome examples and some suggested activities; it also provides a grid that you can use for this activity. Caution: This activity is just to get you started thinking about the guidance curriculum, but this is such an important element that we devote an entire chapter to it (see Chapter 6).

Individual Planning

Individual planning addresses the process of helping students develop their own life plans to reach their fullest potential. Methods used include individual appraisal, advising, and placement. Individual planning does not necessarily mean that the counselor meets with the student one-on-one. It does mean that the best method of meeting individual students' needs is used. Often this is within a classroom or with a group of peers.

Learning Outcome: Students need to appreciate their own diversity and that of others.

Grade Level	Course	Community	Classroom or Group
K–2			K, 1, and 2 Singing
3–5			3, 4, and 5 Singing and Art
6–8	Integrated Arts	Parents' Night	All classes
9–10	English, Social Science	Submit to Local News	All classes
11–12	Language Arts	Community Evening	All classes

Learning Outcome: Each student will graduate with a completed portfolio.

Grade Level	Course	Community	Classroom or Group
K–2			
3–5			
6–8			
9–10			
11–12			

Figure 4.2 Learning outcomes example

Activity 4.2   Determining the Best Setting

In three groups, develop lists of individual planning needs of students. Use individual appraisal, individual advisement, and placement as general headings. List as many activities as possible in which appraisal, advisement, and placement occur within the school. Label each activity as one-on-one, small group, or classroom. You may want to develop a grid similar to the one in Activity 4.1. Share your lists in the large group.

Responsive Services

Counselors traditionally are trained to respond to students' needs, whether the students are in crisis or simply seeking information. The *responsive services* component of the program goes beyond the counseling expertise of the counselor and reaches out to the helping expertise of the faculty, the administration, and others who have skills that lend themselves to counseling and consultation in a school setting. For example, many classroom teachers and some administrators have earned certification as school counselors but have chosen to use their skills in the classrooms or in the principal's office; therefore, they can become important resources in providing responsive services.

The emphasis on responsive services in this model is on prevention as well as intervention. Whether the counselor is working with an individual, a small group, or in a classroom, or consulting with a teacher or parent on behalf of the student, problem-solving and decision-making skills are emphasized so that students develop coping skills that can be used in a variety of settings.

Activity 4.3   The Solution-Based Model

The solution-based model (Figure 4.3) is a well-known method of working with a student in a responsive services mode. Using the solution-based model, create a responsive services scenario with which the school counselor is likely to be presented. Working in

The Solution-Based Model

This format can be used with teachers and students, parents and students, and administrators and students. What follows is a format for a solution-based interview that we have found useful with "problem" children and whoever made the referral. The interview with the child usually takes about 20 minutes; the interview with the referring person usually takes about 5–10 minutes and can be done over the phone or in person.

Basic assumptions of the solution-based model:

- Accept the view of the student as reality for him/her.
- Flow with that view.
- Name the problem which has to be solved.
- Search for exceptions to the problem condition.
- Use exceptions to find solutions.
- Compliment the student for willingness to confront the problem by talking to you and for any effort made toward solving the problem already.
- Compliment the referral person for hard work on the problem so far. (For involuntary clients: Who made you come here? What do they say has to be different?)

Part 1 (with student)

1. What has to be different as s result of you talking with me? What is your goal?

2. When was the last time you did this even a little bit better than now? (Ask this several times)

3. What were you doing differently at that time? (Need several answers to this question)

4. On a scale of 1 to 10, with 1 being not so sure and 10 being very sure, how sure are you that you could do some of these things again if you really wanted to?

5. How likely is it that you will be able to do some of these things again?

Part 2 (with parent, teacher, etc.)

1. Acknowledge their hard work on problem so far, dedication to solve problem, etc.
   What is the minimal change you can accept from this child?

2. When was the last time you found this child doing just a little bit better or a little more of what you wanted?

3. What was this child doing differently at that time? (Need several answers to this question.)

4. What do you think you were doing that helped this child to do better at times? What would the child say you were doing that helped him/her at the time?

5. How willing are you to do these things to help this child again?

Figure 4.3 A school interview in two parts

Source: From *A School Interview in Two Parts: The Solution-Based Model,* by J. K. Gilkey and I. K. Berg, 1991, Milwaukee, WI: Brief Family Therapy Center. Reprinted with permission of the authors.

After we have interviewed each party involved in the problem (in the solution-based model), we accept each person's view of the problem as reality for him or her, and we compliment each person on his or her efforts to solve the problem thus far. We refrain from making judgments on how that has been done. We then give each a task to do; if each has tried several things that have worked in part, we send them out to do more of those things and to come back or call and tell us how those worked.

If nothing has worked even a little bit or not too many things have worked, we send each party out to study themselves to see what works better in the next few days or a week. We then see them again or talk with them to get this information. *Trust the pace and the path of the client.*

Figure 4.3 Continued

triads, one person will be the counselor, one the student, and one the teacher or parent. Work for approximately twenty minutes to resolve the presenting problem.

Be aware that, in creating your responsive services component, you need to develop and keep an up-to-date list of available referral programs, services, and individual providers. Consultation and referral services can often be as powerful as direct counseling services for meeting students' needs.

System Support/Program Management

System support or *program management,* viewed sometimes as the core of a school counselor's responsibility and sometimes as a necessary evil, is as important as the other components of the program. Often it is considered narrowly as the day-to-day operation of the guidance area. It includes but is not limited to research and development, public awareness and support, professional development, committees and advisory boards, and community outreach. Counselors need a good grasp of program management to maintain inner control of their services. The person designated as the head counselor should take the lead responsibility for convening the counselors on a regular basis to maintain communication among them and between them and other professionals. We are not including a specific activity for this area of the Missouri model because we want to point out that this entire book is about the systems support/program management component of the program.

THE MULTIDIMENSIONAL MODEL

In Chapter 2 we asked you to continually include the human factor as you plan and implement your comprehensive school counseling program. As you examine the multidimensional model (Figure 4.4), remember that the most important parts of any program are the human beings for whom the program is designed. The multidimensional model illustrates that the "human factor" is the glue that keeps the system together.

Organization

The organizational design is the counselor's method of envisioning and depicting the finished product, or the optimally functioning program, before encountering the first student. It is a work design or operational structure that helps improve productivity.

The planning-supporting-implementing-operating-evaluating (PSIOE) design illustrated in the lower left part of the cube shown in Figure 4.4 is an organizational format suggested by a national project entitled "Legislative Provisions for the Development of

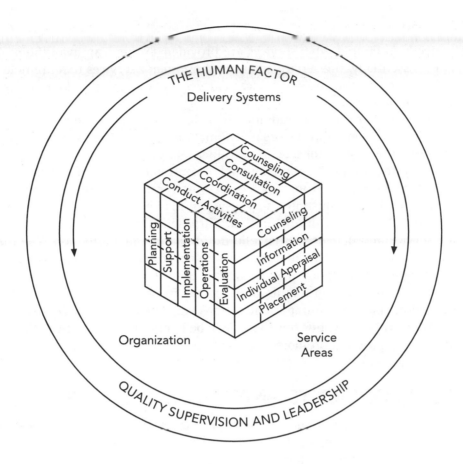

Figure 4.4 Multidimensional model of guidance program management

Comprehensive Community-Based Career Guidance Programs" (Drier, Jones, & Jones, 1985). The PSIOE format provides a comprehensive framework in which to perceive program organization.

Delivery Systems: The Four Cs Model

With each new professional encounter, a counselor must determine the most appropriate intervention strategy. Counselors do not "just do counseling." Since the mid-1960s, counselors have been indoctrinated with the idea that "three Cs" constitute the major functions performed by a counselor (counseling, consultation, and coordination). The multidimensional model, however, proposes a fourth "C" (conducting activities). This function explains the intervention approaches in which counselors typically deliver services that address the needs of their clients but do not fall under the other three categories (for example, producing newsletters). Of course, the most prominent activity under this fourth C is delivering the guidance curriculum lessons in classrooms. Counseling and conducting activities are *direct* delivery systems, whereas consultation and coordination are *indirect* interventions.

Program managers need to remember that these four Cs are not always mutually exclusive. They may, at times, complement each other, and occasionally two or more delivery systems may be employed with the same clients.

Service Areas

The public needs to be told what services are provided so they can avail themselves of these services. Essentially, the service areas are those major services that are held out to the public for their use and for which clear-cut descriptions are developed to promote maximum appropriate use.

Follow-up, another function traditionally included under service areas, is absorbed by the evaluation component of the organizational model or is seen as an extension of a counseling intervention. It is not seen as a distinct service.

In summary, the multidimensional model of counseling program management provides a conceptual framework from which one counselor or an entire program or agency may operate. It graphically illustrates how a system may be viewed as a whole and also how its parts, which are fairly distinct in their purpose and function, interrelate.

All the service and delivery systems do not demand equal attention. The managerial situation that presents itself will dictate where proper emphasis should be placed.

Overlapping and duplication may occur, but the model minimizes these problems. Any overlapping or duplication that does occur may illustrate the complementary roles that such functions play. More importantly, however, this type of model decreases the possibility that essential functions or services will be overlooked or omitted. This systematic look at the total program promotes the creation of programs that are comprehensive, efficient, and accountable.

NEW DEVELOPMENTS—NATIONAL MODELS

Since the first edition of this handbook was published (VanZandt & Hayslip, 1994), a number of initiatives have emerged from national organizations and are being adapted into state and local guidelines or frameworks.

National Standards for School Counseling Programs

In 1997, the American School Counselor Association (ASCA) introduced the National Standards for School Counseling Programs (see Figure 4.5).

National standards are what ASCA believes to be the essential elements of a quality and effective school counseling program. The standards address program content and the knowledge, attitudes, and skill competencies that all students will develop as a result of participating in a school counseling program. (Campbell & Dahir, 1997, p. 3)

National Career Development Guidelines

The National Career Development Guidelines (Figure 4.6) provide hierarchically arranged competencies at the elementary, middle, high school, and adult levels, illustrating that career development is a lifelong venture. As stated in the introduction to the guidelines, "they provide a blueprint of career development competencies that children, youth, and adults should master, and identify standards or indicators of evidence that individuals have attained these competencies."

SCANS

During the early 1990s, the Secretary's Commission on Achieving Necessary Skills (SCANS) (Figure 4.7) was directed to advise the U.S. Secretary of Labor on the level of skills required for young people to meet the demands of a global economy and a workforce that was increasingly dependent on technology. The commission explored the current situation

National Standards For School Counseling Programs

The purpose of a counseling program in a school setting is to promote and enhance the learning process. To that end, the School Counseling Program facilitates Student Development in three broad areas: Academic Development, Career Development, and Personal/Social Development.

I. Academic Development

Standard A: Students will acquire the attitudes, knowledge, and skills that contribute to effective learning in school and across the life span.

Standard B: Students will complete school with the academic preparation essential to choose from a wide range of substantial postsecondary options, including college.

Standard C: Students will understand the relationship of academics to the world of work, and to life at home and in the community.

II. Career Development

Standard A: Students will acquire the skills to investigate the world of work in relation to knowledge of self and to make informed career decisions.

Standard B: Students will employ strategies to achieve future career success and satisfaction.

Standard C: Students will understand the relationship between personal qualities, education and training, and the world of work.

III. Personal/Social Development

Standard A: Students will acquire the attitudes, knowledge, and interpersonal skills to help them understand and respect self and other.

Standard B: Students will make decisions, set goals, and take necessary action to achieve these goals.

Standard C: Students will understand safety and survival skills.

Figure 4.5 ASCA national standards for school counseling programs

Source: Reprinted with the permission of the American School Counselor Association.

and future needs in American schools and the American workplace through extensive discussions, interviews, and meetings with business owners, public employers, unions, and workers and supervisors in shops, plants, and stores. The prevailing message from their research was:

> Good jobs will increasingly depend on people who can put knowledge to work. What we found was disturbing: more than half our young people leave school without the knowledge or foundation required to find and hold a good job. These young people will pay a very high price. They face the bleak prospects of dead-end work interrupted only by periods of unemployment. (SCANS, 1992, p. xv)

The message was not intended so much as a portent of doom but as a call to action. A major recommendation of the SCANS report was that schools find ways to promote "workplace know-how" that would lead to effective job performance. This know-how has two elements: competencies and a foundation. Figure 4.7 charts these elements.

National Career Development Guidelines

Elementary	Middle/Junior High School	High School	Adult
Self-Knowledge			
Knowledge of the importance of self-concept	Knowledge of the influence of a positive self-concept	Understanding the influence of a positive self-concept	Skills to maintain a positive self-concept
Skills to positively interact with others	Skills to interact with others	Skills to interact positively with others	Skills to maintain effective behaviors
Awareness of the importance of growth and change	Knowledge of the importance of growth and change	Understanding the impact of growth and development	Understanding developmental changes and transitions
Educational and Occupational Exploration			
Awareness of the benefits of educational achievement	Knowledge of the benefits of educational achievement to career opportunities	Understanding the relationship between educational achievement and career planning	Skills to enter and participate in education and training
Awareness of the relationship between work and learning	Understanding the relationship between work and learning	Understanding the need for positive attitudes toward work and learning	Skills to participate in work and life-long learning
Skills to understand and use career information	Skills to locate, understand, and use career information	Skills to locate, evaluate, and interpret career information	Skills to locate, evaluate, and interpret career information
Awareness of the importance of personal responsibility and good work habits	Knowledge of skills necessary to seek and obtain jobs	Skills to prepare to seek, obtain, maintain, and change jobs	Skills to prepare to seek, obtain, maintain, and change jobs
Awareness of how work relates to the needs and functions of society	Understanding how work relates to the needs and functions of the economy and society	Understanding how societal needs and functions influence the nature and structure of work	Understanding how the needs and functions of society influence the nature and structure of work

Figure 4.6

Reprinted with permission of NOICC.

Career Planning

Understanding how to make decisions	Skills to make decisions	Skills to make decisions	Skills to make decisions
Awareness of the interrelationship of life roles	Knowledge of the interrelationship of life roles	Understanding of the interrelationship of life roles	Understanding the impact of work on in-dividual and family life
Awareness of different occupations and changing male/female roles	Knowledge of different occupations and changing male/female roles	Understanding the continuous changes in male/female roles	Understanding the continuing changes in male/female roles
Awareness of the career planning process	Understanding the process of career planning	Skills in career planning	Skills to make career transitions

Figure 4.6 Continued

SCANS Competencies

Resources
- Allocates time
- Allocates money
- Allocates materials and facility resources
- Allocates human resources

Interpersonal
- Participates as team member
- Teaches others
- Serves clients/customers
- Exercises leadership
- Negotiates
- Works with cultural diversity

Information
- Acquires and evaluates information
- Organizes and maintains information
- Interprets and communicates information

Systems
- Understands systems
- Monitors and corrects performance
- Improves and designs systems

Technology
- Selects technology
- Applies technology to task
- Maintains and troubleshoots technology

Foundation
BASIC SKILLS
- Reading
- Writing
- Arithmetic/Mathematics
- Listening
- Speaking

THINKING SKILLS
- Creative thinking
- Decision making
- Problem solving
- Seeing things in the mind's eye

PERSONAL QUALITIES
- Responsibility
- Self-esteem
- Sociability
- Self-management
- Integrity/honesty

Conclusion: The workforce of tomorrow requires that schools teach a variety of skills that go beyond the basic reading, writing, and arithmetic. Students must now be prepared to cooperate in problem solving and be effective communicators.

Figure 4.7

Activity 4.4 Applying National Models

As you review these models that have implications for your comprehensive developmental school counseling programs, try to determine answers to the following:

1. What are some similarities?

2. What are some differences?

3. As your group is developing its model, which of the models or which parts of the models would you use or not use? Why?

Activity 4.5 Creating a Model

Within your groups, discuss the strengths and weaknesses of the models presented thus far. Now, using the best of these, plus others that you may have read about in your texts, choose or create a model for your group. Do not worry if some of the elements fit nicely into the scheme of your model while others blend or cut across lines. Career development, for example, probably fits just about anywhere in the graphic. Crisis intervention appears, at first glance, to fit into responsive services; however, depending upon how the crises present themselves, crisis intervention may also fit into curriculum (preventative model).

Summary

In this chapter, you have had an opportunity to examine several program models. Although there are other models available, these are the ones that we find are most complementary to the comprehensive developmental model that you will be creating in this handbook.

References

Campbell, C. A., & Dahir, C. A. (1997). *The national standards for school counseling programs.* Alexandria, VA: American School Counselor Association.

Drier, H. Jones, B., & Jones, L. (1985). *Legislative provisions for the development of comprehensive community-based career guidance programs.* Wooster, OH: Bell and Howell.

Gysbers, N. C., & Henderson, P. (1988). *Developing and managing your school guidance program.* Alexandria, VA: American Association for Counseling and Development.

Secretary's Commission on Achieving Necessary Skills (SCANS). (1992). *Learning a living: A blueprint for high performance.* Washington, DC: U.S. Department of Labor.

VanZandt, C. E., & Hayslip, J. B. (1994). *Your comprehensive school guidance and counseling program: A handbook of practical activities.* White Plains, NY: Longman.

For Further Reading

Carr, J. V., Hayslip, J. B., & Randall, J. (1987). *New Hampshire comprehensive guidance and counseling program: A model for program development.* Plymouth, NH: Plymouth State College.

Gilkey, J. K., & Berg, I. K. (1991). *A school interview in two parts: The solution-based model.* Milwaukee, WI: Brief Family Therapy Center.

Kobylarz, L., & Hayslip, J. (1996). National career development guidelines: K–adult handbook. Stillwater, OK: NOICC Training Support Center.

Myrick, R. D. (1987). *Developmental guidance and counseling.* Minneapolis, MN: Educational Media Corp.

VanZandt, C. E. (1993). *Multidimensional model of guidance program management.* Gorham, ME: University of Southern Maine.

VanZandt, Z., & Buchan, B. A. (1997). *Lessons for life: Career development activities library: Vol. 1. Elementary grades.* West Nyack, NY: The Center for Applied Research in Education.

VanZandt, Z., & Buchan, B. A. (1997). *Lessons for life: Career development activities library: Vol. 2. Secondary grades.* West Nyack, NY: The Center for Applied Research in Education.

Textbooks

Arredondo, P. (1996). *Successful diversity management initiatives: A blueprint for planning and implementation.* Thousand Oaks, CA: Sage.

Baker, S. (1992). *School counseling for the twenty-first century.* New York: Macmillan.

Bridges, W. (1992). *Transitions: Making sense of life's changes.* Melrose Park, CA: Addison-Wesley.

Brown, D., & Brooks, L. (1991). *Career counseling techniques.* Boston: Allyn & Bacon.

Burgess, D. G., & Dedmond, R. M. (Eds.). *Quality leadership and the professional school counselor.* Alexandria, VA: American School Counselor Association.

Coy, D. R., Cole, C., Huey, W. C., & Sears, S. J. (Eds.). (1991). *Toward the transformation of secondary school counseling.* Alexandria, VA: American School Counselor Association.

Ettinger, J. (Ed.). (1995). *Improved decision making in a changing world* (2nd ed.). Garrett Park, MD: Garrett Park Press.

Feller, R., & Walz, G. (1996). *Career transitions in turbulant times: Exploring work, learning and careers.* Alexandria, VA: American School Counselor Association.

Gysbers, N. C. (Ed.). (1990). *Comprehensive guidance programs that work.* Ann Arbor, MI: University of Michigan. ERIC Counseling and Personnel Services Clearing House.

Gysbers, N. C., & Associates. (1984). *Designing careers.* San Francisco: Jossey-Bass.

Gysbers, N. C., & Henderson, P. (1994). *Developing and managing your school guidance program.* Alexandria, VA: American Counseling Association.

Gysbers, N. C., & Moore, E. J. (1987). *Career counseling: Skills and techniques for practitioners.* Englewood Cliffs, NJ: Prentice-Hall.

Hansen, L. S. (1997). *Integrative life planning: Critical tasks for career development and changing life patterns.* San Francisco: Jossey-Bass.

Herr, E. L., & Cramer, S. H. (1996). *Career guidance and counseling through the life span: Systematic approaches.* Boston: Little, Brown.

Herring, R. (1998).*Career counseling in schools: A multicultural and developmental approach.* Alexandria, VA: American Counseling Association.

Kapes, J. T., & Mastie, M. M. (1994). *A counselor's guide to career assessment instruments* (3rd ed.). Alexandria, VA: American Counseling Association.

Leah, D., & Liebowitz, Z. B. (Eds.). (1991). *Adult career development: Concepts, Issues, and practices* (2nd ed.). Alexandria, VA: American Counseling Association.

Lee, C. C., & Richardson, B. L. (Eds.). (1991). *Multicultural issues in counseling: New approaches to diversity.* Alexandria, VA: American Counseling Association.

Liebowitz, Z. B., Farren, C., & Kaye, B. (1986). *Designing career development systems.* San Francisco: Jossey-Bass.

McDaniels, C. (1989). *The changing workplace.* San Francisco: Jossey-Bass.

McDaniels, C., & Gysbers, N. C. (1992). *Counseling for career development: Theories, resources, and practice.* San Francisco: Jossey-Bass.

Myrick, R. D. (1994). *Developmental guidance and counseling: A practical approach.* Minneapolis, MN: Educational Media.

Paisley, P., & Hubbard, C. (1994). *Developmental school counseling programs: From theory to practice.* Alexandria, VA: American Counseling Association.

Resnick, L. B., & Wirt, J. (1995). *Linking school and work: Roles for standards and assessments.* Alexandria, VA: American Vocational Association.

Schlossberg, N. (1984). *Counseling adults in transition: Linking practice with theory.* New York: Springer.

Schmidt, J. J. (1997). *Counseling in Schools: Essential services and comprehensive programs* (3rd ed.). Boston, MA: Allyn & Bacon.

Sharf, R. S. (1992). *Applying career development theory to counseling.* Pacific Grove, CA: Brooks/Cole.

VanZandt, C. E., & Hayslip, J. B. (1994). *Your comprehensive school guidance and counseling program: A handbook of practical activities.* White Plains, NY: Longman.

Yost, E. B., & Corbishley, M. A. (1987). *Career counseling: A psychological approach.* San Francisco: Jossey-Bass.

Zunker, V. G. (1998). *Career counseling: Applied concepts for life planning* (5th ed.). Pacific Grove, CA: Brooks/Cole.

Zunker, V. G. (1998). *Using assessment results for career development* (5th ed.). Pacific Grove, CA: Brooks/Cole.

Reflections on Chapter 4

1. What's going on in your group?

2. What models are favored by your group for creating the most comprehensive developmental school guidance and counseling program?

3. How is your model different from the others in this chapter?

4. How complete is the graphic depiction of your model? Will it explain your program to your school board?

5. What questions do you have for yourself, your group members, or your facilitator?

6. Notes:

 **Chapter 5**

Determining Program Priorities and Focus

In *Alice in Wonderland*, the Cheshire Cat said, "If you don't know where you're going, you'll end up somewhere else." Not only do counselors need to know their priorities; the other members of the school and community also need to know them. In this chapter, we explain the procedures we believe will help determine your program priorities and assist you in informing the rest of the school and community about your program.

Determining program priorities requires a carefully orchestrated system of identifying the needs of your community. Needs assessments are but *one* piece, albeit a major piece, of a complex method of arriving at program priorities. It is important to keep in mind that a school counselor's knowledge and training also must figure into the decisions. We are the only professionals in the schools who have been trained to develop comprehensive developmental school counseling programs; therefore, we have the greatest expertise for addressing the complexities and intricacies of a well-functioning program. We must bring a global understanding of the philosophical, theoretical, and paradigmatic models that have shaped our professional orientation, and use those models for understanding the needs of our constituents. Essentially, then, we need to retain ownership of this management process while also honoring the significance of input from "those who are responsible for or affected by the program."

SOCIOLOGICAL ASSESSMENT

A significant ingredient in the recipe for priority setting is a sociological assessment of the community. Each community has a unique personality and its own set of particular characteristics, norms, and issues. A community's ethnic heritage or economic circumstances, for instance, may impose certain pressures or influences on the students in its schools. An example might include a community with a high dropout rate *and* low scores on achievement tests. The students probably would not rate dropout prevention as a high priority. Counselors, however, can provide critical information to help community members see the significance of the combination and add this information to other data that are compiled to determine program needs.

Activity 5.1   Assessing the Community

Figure 5.1, Know Your Community, provides a survey form that may be used for gathering information about the sociological factors that contribute to a school's areas of need.

1. For those who are creating fictitious results for the sake of expediting the planning process as part of an educational exercise, this is a good time to name and describe your fictitious school district. Describe the type of community, how many schools are in your district, how many students are enrolled, the number of school counselors, and so on. (It is all right to be idealistic or to create sociological problems that meet the unique characteristics you agree upon.) Use Figure 5.1 to identify the important characteristics that will be essential for your planning. Agreeing on this information may make the planning task more focused.

I.   Descriptive data
    A. Brief history
    B. Geography
    C. Population
    D. Type of community
        1. Value of property
        2. Religious makeup
        3. Minority and ethnic groups
        4. Socioeconomic makeup
    E. Unique characteristics
II. Occupational and industrial data
    A. Type of industry
        1. Educational requirements for employment
        2. Role of unions
    B. Employment rates
    C. Occupational classification
    D. Training programs
III. Power structure
    A. Financial
    B. Political and governmental
    C. Educational
    D. Religious
    E. Underlying authority
IV. Services
    A. Related educational and psychological
    B. Municipal
        1. Health
        2. Welfare
        3. Protective
        4. Recreation
    C. Organizations
    D. Mass communications and media
V.   Attitudes and values
    A. Toward education
    B. Toward particular schools
    C. Toward crimes and morality
    D. Concerning social strata

Figure 5.1 Know your community

2. For those who are working with actual school settings, use the form in Figure 5.1 to identify both the demographic information and the sociological factors that need consideration in your deliberations.

NEEDS ASSESSMENT

We believe it is imperative that a comprehensive needs assessment be conducted before you begin to set or change priorities. When you conduct a needs assessment, you must remember that you are not relinquishing control of your program; you are merely asking for input. Furthermore, there is no way that you could ever honor the requests of everyone who states an opinion about what topics need to be addressed. Therefore, you must inform people about what a needs assessment will and will *not* do.

First, a needs assessment seeks opinions about the *content* of the program. If you are talking about what people's needs are, you should focus on the issues in their lives that are the most urgent. Once you start venturing off into questions about whether you should be doing individual or group counseling, classroom guidance, or whatever, you are getting away from determining needs and instead are asking people to tell you how you should be managing your program. True, it never hurts to get a little advice on such matters, but not from everyone in the community! That is not the purpose of a needs assessment. Be careful about mixing apples and oranges. It should be easy to determine which topics demand the most attention in your program by maintaining a focus on what people believe to be their needs.

Make it clear that you cannot deliver services to meet all the needs identified. The needs assessment helps determine the *priority* areas that will be addressed by your program while also determining which needs will have to be handled by some other programs—or perhaps not handled at all.

CREATING THE NEEDS ASSESSMENT

As with any kind of assessment, you should be concerned primarily with the content validity of your needs assessment. Listing all your favorite counseling tasks or group counseling topics does not create a valid needs assessment. The more you rely on the professional literature to guide your choices, the more validity you should be able to expect from your instrument.

Figure 5.2 provides an example of a needs assessment that lists several topics for a high school counseling program. Note that blank spaces are provided for people to add their own topics. The weighted priorities make it possible for topics to be identified both by the number of times they are cited, as well as by the relative importance they hold for those who are listing them.

By differentiating the responses of parents, teachers, students, and community members, the counseling program is able to discern whether various groups see similar priority needs or whether different perspectives will need to be addressed in program planning. This particular needs assessment was used in a school where students were also asked to identify their grade level at the top of the page. An interesting finding was that suicide was a major issue in the eleventh grade, but barely made anyone's list in the twelfth grade. Such a finding caused the counselors and administrators to take a careful look at the reasons why. Also, the finding helped them know where to focus their attention (certainly during the junior year, but before then as well).

Activity 5.2 Identifying Needs

1. Using Figure 5.2, Guidance Program Needs Assessment, complete the needs assessment, according to the directions you are given, for either a fictitious high school or one in your district.
   a. Tabulate the results for your group.
   b. Identify what *appear to be* the priority needs, starting with the item with the highest score, then listing the items in descending order. Write these priority need areas on a separate sheet of paper, and use the list as a working document for developing your program's final priorities.
   c. Discuss the findings. Explore some of the possible reasons that certain items received such high scores. Ask questions or seek clarification about data that cause concerns or raise issues.
2. Explore what changes will be needed to make the needs assessment applicable to a middle or elementary school setting.
3. Suggest changes you would make to improve the needs assessment in Figure 5.2, keeping in mind the cautions mentioned earlier in this chapter.
4. Generate needs assessment spreadsheets or data summaries that will allow your planning group to view the district's needs from a K–12 perspective and to proceed with the development of program priorities and outcomes.
5. Discuss the *procedures* your group will use for finalizing the priority list, including decisions about which content areas will *not* be addressed.
6. According to the compiled data, what are the priority needs of your school counseling program? Share these needs in your group so that everyone is in agreement with the final product.

A reminder: The needs assessment data provide information about how others see your program. Parents, teachers, students, and community members may have different ratings for how service areas meet needs. Your responsibility is to determine which areas need the most attention.

TIME AND TASK ANALYSIS

Concurrent with the needs assessment, a thorough time and task analysis should be conducted by the guidance staff. This is an instrument used by counselors to survey and analyze the distribution of their time and the tasks that they are performing. Sample time and task analysis forms are included in many textbooks (Gysbers & Henderson, 1988; Myrick, 1987). It is important to have this time and task analysis completed and ready to use along with your needs assessment results when you meet with your planning committee. (Students will need to estimate figures.) We suggest that the time and task analysis cover your guidance curriculum, individual planning, responsive services, and system support or program management tasks. In addition, you should factor in the time that is spent on nonguidance functions. This information will be very important when you analyze your data and determine new program priorities. If you can demonstrate that you are performing certain functions that could be more economically or more appropriately done by others, you will be able to spend your time and your energy on programs that have the greatest need.

Activity 5.3 School Board Summons

Your local school board has requested a description of counselor activities for the previous academic year. You suspect that the board's motive is to cut one of the four positions

Guidance Program Needs Assessment

The counselors would like your help in planning the school counseling program. Please read the directions and give your honest feedback. Do *not* sign this form; just circle whether you are a student, parent, teacher, or community member. Thank you for your cooperation.

Student   Parent   Teacher   Community Member

I.   The following list names some topics that might be addressed in a school counseling program. Even though all of these topics might sound interesting or valuable, we are trying to find out what students, parents, teachers, and community members consider to be the *most* important topics. We would like you to rank order the top 10 topics that you feel would be most valuable in terms of your own needs or the needs of the whole school. Put the number 10 next to the topic that you feel would be most valuable, the number 9 by the next most valuable, and so on down to the number 1. Do not list more than 10. If you have some suggestions that are not on the list, place them in the spaces that have been provided and include your suggestions in your top 10 ratings. Your results will be that your highest scores equal your highest priorities.

1. __10__ Help with educational planning, graduation requirements, and choosing courses

2. __10__   2. __7__ Self-awareness and self-concept   10

3. _____ Career decision making

4. _____ Help for special learning needs

5. __2__   5. _____ Appreciation of diverse populations

6. __4__   6. _____ Peer pressure

7. __4__ Substance abuse

8. __1__   8. _____ Resolving conflicts and making compromises

9. _____ Problem solving

10. __9__   10. __8__ Coping with difficult situations (divorce, loss, moving, new school adjustment)

11. __1__ Suicide

12. _____ Job-seeking and job-keeping skills

13. _____ Study skills

14. __3__   14. _____ Decision-making skills

15. _____ Help for transfer students

16. _____ Special enrichment programs (Boys'/Girls' State, Talent Search, Upward Bound)

17. __6__   17. _____ Orientation to guidance services and how to use them

18. __7__   18. _____ Exploration of personal goals and aspirations

19. _____ Help with postsecondary options, admissions, applications, recommendations, and financial aid

20. __2__ Dating/relationship issues

21. __6__ Family relationships

22. __5__ Peer relationships

23. __8__   23. __9__ Social adjustment (making friends, getting along with people)

24. 5   24. _____ School/classroom behavior

Figure 5.2

25. _____ Sexual issues

26. __3__ Physical or sexual abuse or neglect concerns

27. _____

28. _____

II. Program services. Typically, issues and topics are addressed through the six major service areas listed below with samples of the services. After reading the list, circle the appropriate number to rate the service areas according to the emphasis they should receive in the total school counseling program.

4	3	2	1
Top Priority	Moderate Priority	Fairly Low Priority	Very Low Priority

4 3 2 1   1. COUNSELING SERVICE (individual and group counseling, support groups, referral to agencies)

4 3 2 1   2. APPRAISAL SERVICE (achievement tests, career interest inventories, special needs assessment, personality inventories, portfolios)

4 3 2 1   3. INFORMATION SERVICE (student records, handbooks, computerized data programs, postsecondary catalogs)

4 3 2 1   4. PLACEMENT SERVICE (enrichment programs, college admissions, course selection, career advising, referral to agencies)

4 3 2 1   5. CONSULTATION SERVICE (conferences with parents, teachers, and administrators; student assistance programs)

4 3 2 1   6. CURRICULAR SERVICES (organization of materials for classroom teacher adoption, group and classroom presentation of guidance topics)

Figure 5.2 Continued

Source: Developed by University of Southern Maine students, summer 1991.

in your district program, which has one elementary counselor for K–6, two secondary school counselors for 7–12, and one school adjustment counselor for K–12. School enrollment for K–12 is 1,200 students and is growing by about 25 students per year. Base your presentation to the school board on an analysis of the time spent by counseling personnel on various activities. Use whatever support or information you can from other individuals in your school and community.

1. How will you present the information to the school board so that it is "meaningful" in terms of their decision-making needs?

2. Process this activity as a group.

   a. Without keeping records, how easy is it to explain how a counselor spends his or her time?

   b. Considering the amount of time you suggested was being spent on various activities, how impressed do you think the school board would be? _____ Why?

FORMATIVE EVALUATION

Another piece of the priority-setting process evolves from an ongoing evaluation of the school counseling program. As you regularly assess the effectiveness of the programs, services, and interventions you have delivered, you will receive feedback that will help you improve. Sometimes you may even receive information that suggests eliminating one of your projects. Letting go of familiar turf is one of the more difficult challenges for many counselors, but it needs to be done.

Often, school counseling programs submit end-of-the-year reports to summarize their accomplishments and provide data for school district documents. Although such reports are usually considered summative in nature, they also can provide formative information when combined with the sociological information, needs assessment data, and time and task analysis. More information about program evaluation is provided in Chapter 12.

PROFESSIONAL INTEGRITY

As was mentioned in the introduction to this chapter, counselors need to determine program priorities in the context of professional models of excellence. Chapter 4 provided examples of such models that can be used for creating a conceptual framework for program development. Sharing resources like the *National Standards for School Counseling Programs* (Campbell & Dahir, 1997) with a planning team can enlighten members about the expectations of the profession, thus maintaining the integrity of the profession while inviting input about program priorities. The resources offered in the appendices of this handbook also can be used to educate those who will be involved in the decisions that will shape the direction of the school counseling program.

Activity 5.4   Sharing Information

As a group, come to a consensus about the *one* article or handout that would be used as a frame of reference for a planning team or steering committee comprised of both counselors and noncounselors. Consider any information from courses you have taken, professional journals, state or national publications, or parts of this book.

Title of the resource: _____

Why was it chosen?

SYNTHESIZING THE INFORMATION

Now that you have collected information about your community and school needs and have analyzed this information in the context of a conceptual framework and other supporting information, it is time to create a final list of priorities.

Activity 5.5   Finalizing the Program Priorities

1. What method of decision making will the group use to finalize its decision? _____ Is consensus preferred over majority rule? _____ Do you have procedures for seeking compromises? _____ Should only the steering committee be able to vote? _____ If others can vote, how do you include them? _____

2. Develop a procedure for determining the final list of priorities. Discuss the importance of having ownership of the final product. Why is ownership of the priority list a critical factor in the successful development of the school counseling program?

- group consensus + data
*when appropriate

BECOMING FOCUSED

Now that the program priorities have been determined, it is important to turn your attention to the development of a mission statement for your program. A mission statement sets out to explain what the program ultimately hopes to accomplish by describing the scope and depth of the program you will create. It is a concise yet profound statement that encompasses the major philosophical beliefs underlying the program's operation and the school's aspirations for students who participate in the services and interventions that are offered by the program. It is best to limit the mission statement to no more than five or six sentences.

The school counseling program's mission statement should be consistent with the school's mission statement, yet it should be distinct enough to highlight the uniqueness of the program. Often a mission statement for a school counseling program will include terms such as *developmental, comprehensive, K–12, cooperative,* or *empowering.* The challenge is to use strong and optimistic language without employing too many buzzwords that defy definition.

Activity 5.6 Create a Mission Statement

1. Use the brainstorming technique to identify all the potential terms that the planning team members would like to see in the mission statement.

2. Discuss the list of terms and decide whether some terms can be combined or incorporated under others.
3. If possible, use consensus to agree upon the final list of terms that will be included in the mission statement.

4. Have one person in the group who has excellent writing skills draft a mission statement that does not exceed five sentences (fewer is better). The person may need to be given time away from the group meeting to create the draft copy. It will also be important for this person to understand that this mission statement is a *working draft* and that it will more than likely change—sometimes dramatically. Therefore, the author should not become too "wedded" to his or her words, but should remain flexible and work with the group to create a statement that is acceptable to everyone.
5. Try not to spend an inordinate amount of time on this task, but give it a good effort, then bring the statement out again on a regular basis as you add detail to your comprehensive plan. It is perfectly appropriate to refine the mission statement as the program outcomes and strategies become clearer.

A FOCUS ON OUTCOMES

As a final means of creating a focus for your school counseling program, we will now direct our attention to the development of outcomes. Many people are confused by the distinction between goals and objectives, so it is understandable that many educators have found the term *outcomes* to be user-friendly. Essentially, an outcome states what a person or group of people *will know* or *be able to do*.

Outcomes present their own challenges. Creating a comprehensive school counseling program will require three different kinds of outcomes: program outcomes, student outcomes, and counselor outcomes. The reason we have three different kinds of outcomes refers back to our earlier discussion about accountability. In a comprehensive program, we want the *program* to be accountable for delivering certain services and resources; we want *students* to be accountable for and invested in their educational, social-personal, and career development; and as *counselors,* we need to remain accountable to our profession and to our job responsibilities. Chapter 6, Building Your Curriculum, will take these outcomes one step further as you continue to develop your program.

Activity 5.7   Identifying Outcomes

1. Individually, brainstorm several outcomes for each of the following areas. Keep in mind the program priorities established through your needs assessment analysis and the development of your mission statement. One example is included in each of the following areas, but feel free to eliminate the example if it does not complement your particular program's direction.

Program Outcomes

- The school counseling program will provide up-to-date information resources to assist students in their educational, social-personal, and career decision making.

-

-

-

Student Outcomes

- Each student will graduate with a completed career portfolio. (This will look familiar to you because you worked on this in Chapter 4.)

-

-

-

Counselor Outcomes

- All counselors in the school district will actively participate in monthly counselor supervision sessions.

-

-

-

2. Share your lists in your planning group. Discuss them and clarify the outcomes. On newsprint or on a separate sheet of paper, compile a master list.
3. Eliminate any outcomes that do not complement the program priorities list you generated earlier.
4. Vote (by consensus? by majority?) on the final list of outcomes in each category.

This activity is very important, as it sets the stage for your entire program (and everything else that follows in this book). If you have program outcomes, student outcomes, and counselor outcomes all defined in measurable terms, you will be able to explain your comprehensive developmental program to any and all of your constituents.

You have now completed the most challenging part of creating a comprehensive school counseling program plan. *Congratulations.*

Summary

In this chapter, you have taken a giant step toward changing from a service model to a program model. Conducting a thorough needs assessment provides the "meaningful information" for establishing program priorities. As you present, at this early opportunity, careful and thoughtful data about how and why this change needs to happen, the school board and community will feel empowered and in turn will empower you to continue.

References

Campbell, C. A., & Dahir, C. A. (1997). *National standards for school counseling programs.* Alexandria, VA: American School Counselor Association.

Gysbers, N. C., & Henderson, P. (1988). *Developing and managing your school guidance program.* Alexandria, VA: American Association for Counseling and Development.

Myrick, R. D. (1987) *Developmental guidance and counseling.* Minneapolis, MN: Educational Media Corp.

Reflections on Chapter 5

1. Are the outcomes that you identified in this chapter ones that you wish you had had as a student? Why or why not?

2. How do you feel about the tasks in this chapter? Is anything missing? What changes would you suggest?

3. Identify the stages of group development that have happened during your work on this chapter. Where are you and your group right now in the stages of group development?

4. What questions do you have for yourself, your group members, or the facilitator of your group?

5. Notes:

✢ Chapter 6
Building Your Curriculum

Once you have completed your formal and informal needs assessment, you will need to identify or develop a curriculum that meets the priority needs and focus of your emerging program. Although a great deal of commercial curricula is available, we have found that school personnel also want to develop goals, lessons, and activities that directly relate to their own students.

Members of your steering committee, working with school personnel, will clarify which curriculum outcomes address the identified priorities and whether these will be addressed in classrooms or in small or large groups. After the decision about how each curriculum outcome can best be addressed, you need to find places to infuse these within the total curriculum or the guidance curriculum. Often, you will find that teachers are addressing these outcomes in their classrooms. They may be willing, however, to work with the steering committee to help remove gaps and overlaps. In this case, counselors will be able to act as resources to teaching staff.

An important step in determining which learning outcomes will be taught is to develop a scope and sequence chart for your entire program. Into this chart you need to enter those topics and activities that are already being included and who is teaching them. Then, using your needs assessment data, you need to add those learning outcomes that your team has identified as priorities. Eventually, your planning team will produce a matrix that includes grade levels, curriculum topics, and activities.

We recommend that if the counselor delivers a lesson or learning activity in the classroom, he or she work with the teacher before, during, and after the fact. It is very important that the teacher see the activity as a part of the total school curriculum, and not as an add-on or a squeeze-it-in.

> Guidance activities implemented through classrooms will be carefully coordinated, scheduled well in advance, and well publicized to the administration, teachers, and in many cases, parents. . . . This notice should include a detailed explanation about the purpose of the lesson, how long it will take, and what instructional strategies will be used. (Carr, Brook, Hayslip, Williams, & Zwolinski, 1997)

Figure 6.1 is a suggested scope and sequence chart for determining when and where identified priorities might be included. Using a numbering system will be helpful in identifying outcomes. In this example, middle school counselors will still need to decide at which grade level (5, 6, 7, or 8) lessons will be taught.

The teacher performs an integral role in developing the lesson or learning activity and in the evaluation of the activity. The more the counselor and teacher collaborate on the delivery of the curriculum, the more successful and sustainable it will be.

Learning Outcome	Primary	Intermediate	Middle School	High School
1.1 All students will understand and appreciate their own diversity and that of others.			1.1.8 Students will create a series of murals depicting the cultural diversity in the classroom.	

Figure 6.1 Scope and sequence chart

PROCEDURE FOR DEVELOPING A GUIDANCE CURRICULUM

The following is the procedure to use in developing your guidance curriculum:

1. From your priority list generated from your needs assessment, determine the student outcomes that will address these needs.
2. With the steering committee and with frequent feedback from all school personnel, establish a list of priorities.
3. Identify the most appropriate instructional format for these learning outcomes. Be sure to include extracurricular activities as well as classroom interventions.
4. Develop a scope and sequence matrix chart that clearly indicates when, where, and how the lessons will be developed, introduced, infused, and reinforced. For example, if career awareness activities are introduced in primary and intermediate grades, they need to be reintroduced and/or reinforced at the middle and high school grades.
5. Prominently display a schedule for the entire school year that prompts those who are delivering the program to take proud ownership.
6. Annually review your curriculum and revise lessons based on feedback from teachers and students.

The formats shown in Figure 6.2 demonstrate a range of interventions that can be used in classrooms. Note that the formats are listed on a continuum from those that are more didactic to those that are experiential. Feel free to add your own formats. As you develop your curriculum, ask yourself which format will best achieve the purposes of the curriculum learning outcomes:

Present information: Lectures, readings, discussions, questions and answers
Learn new skills: Demonstrations, questions and answers, simulations

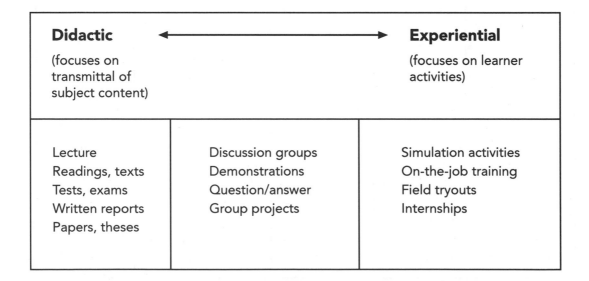

Figure 6.2 Instructional formats appropriate for a guidance curriculum
Source: Adapted from Carr et al. (1997).

Review past behavior: Written reports, questions and answers, discussions, demonstrations

Express feelings: Written reports, questions and answers, discussions, demonstrations, journals

Make plans for the future: Questions and answers, discussions, readings, field tryouts, written reports

BRINGING DIVERSITY PERSPECTIVES INTO THE COUNSELING CURRICULUM

For the first time in the history of the profession, multicultural counseling competencies (Arredondo, Toporek, Brown, Jones, Locke, Sanchez, & Stadler, 1996) have been articulated to guide interpersonal counseling in the context of culture, ethnicity, and race. Educators need to identify and examine their own worldview before they can work with all the students in their school. We are inserting this important element with its accompanying activities at this point in the handbook for your consideration. We also recommend that you have a copy of the manual *Operationalization of the Multicultural Counseling Competencies* (see Figures 6.3 and 6.4). You may choose to pause now and take the pretest from this manual. We have included two versions of it: one for educators (Figure 6.3), and one for students (Figure 6.4). We strongly recommend that you participate in a diversity seminar before you attempt to work with students.

Developing a Lesson Plan/Curriculum Activity

Just as teachers must create lesson plans for their daily instruction, it is also important for school counselors to create lesson plans that facilitate the delivery of the guidance curriculum. The lesson described here is intended to demonstrate a way of connecting the information you have acquired from your needs assessment to a curriculum lesson that you might use in the classroom. For the purpose of this exercise, we are "guessing" that a top priority need is: *Students need to understand and appreciate their own diversity and that of others.*

We assert that a curriculum will have more credibility if it is aligned with national or state standards. In its simplest form, you may want to connect your lessons to just one set of standards. However, we also believe it is possible to demonstrate how certain outcomes are addressed in a multitude of state and national documents. Now, we know that sometimes people are accused of comparing apples and oranges when they attempt to combine different ideas into one basic framework. In trying to align curriculum content with national standards, people often become confused about the various ways concepts are expressed. For the purposes of demonstrating how you can use all the standards-based documents explained in Chapter 4, we are going to attempt to illustrate how you can combine apples with apples (Granny Smith with Cortland with Macintosh). In the previous example about diversity, note the similarity (but difference) in the language used to address diversity:

1. National Standards for School Counseling Programs—Personal/Social Development Standard A: Students will acquire the attitudes, knowledge, and interpersonal skills to help them understand and respect themselves and others.
2. National Career Development Guidelines—Self Knowledge (Middle/Junior High School Level): Skills to interact with others
3. SCANS Competencies—Interpersonal Skills: Works with cultural diversity

Pretest: Multicultural counseling competencies (educator's version)

Please assess on a scale of 1 to 4 (4 = highly aware and 1 = very unaware) at what level of awareness you think you are regarding the following statements. Use the handout.

_____ 1. I am culturally self-aware and sensitive to my own cultural heritage.

_____ 2. I am aware of how my own cultural background and experiences have influenced attitudes, values, and biases about psychological processes.

_____ 3. I am able to recognize the limits of my multicultural competency and expertise.

_____ 4. I can recognize sources of personal discomfort with differences that exist between myself and clients in terms of race, ethnicity, and culture.

_____ 5. I am aware and have specific knowledge about my own racial and cultural heritage and how it personally and professionally affects my definitions and biases of normality/abnormality and the process of counseling.

_____ 6. I am aware of and understand about how oppression, racism, discrimination, and stereotyping affect me personally and in my work.

_____ 7. I am aware of who I am, how I appear, and how I communicate; and how all of this may socially impact on others.

_____ 8. I seek out educational, consultative, and training experiences to improve my understanding and effectiveness in working with culturally different populations. I recognize the limits of my competence and (a) seek consultation, (b) seek further training or education, (c) refer out to more qualified individuals or resources, or (d) engage in a combination of these behaviors.

_____ 9. I constantly seek to understand myself as a racial and cultural being, and actively seek a nonracist identity.

_____10. I am aware of my negative and positive emotional reactions toward other racial and ethnic groups that may prove detrimental to the counseling relationship. I am willing and able to contrast my beliefs and attitudes with those of culturally different clients in a nonjudgmental fashion.

_____11. I am aware of the stereotypes and preconceived notions I hold toward other cultural, linguistic, and racial minorities.

_____12. I have specific knowledge and information about the cultural groups I am working with. I am aware of the life experiences, cultural heritage, and historical background of my culturally different and culturally similar clients.

_____13. I understand how race, culture, ethnicity, etc. may have affected my personality formation, vocational choices, and other life experiences I have had.

_____14. I am aware of and understand about how sociopolitical influences impinge upon my life and that of racial and ethnic minorities, those of immigrant status, and those living under low socioeconomic conditions and/or poverty.

_____15. I keep current with relevant research and the latest findings regarding mental health and mental disorders that affect various ethnic and cultural groups, and seek out educational experiences that enrich my knowledge, understanding, and cross-cultural skills.

_____16. I am actively involved with minority individuals, those culturally different than myself, outside of the counseling setting.

Figure 6.3

Source: Adapted from "Operationalization of the Multicultural Counseling Competencies," by P. Arrendondo, R. Toporek, S. Brown, J. Jones, D. C. Locke, J. Sanchez, & H. Stadler, 1996, *Journal of Multicultural Counseling and Development, 24*. Alexandria, VA: American Counseling Association. Used with permission.

Protect: Diversity learning outcomes
(middle/high school student version)

Please assess on a scale of 1 to 4 (4 = highly aware and 1 = very unaware) at what level of awareness you think you are regarding the following statements.

_____1. I am aware of how my own cultural background and experiences have influenced attitudes, values, and biases in my everyday life.

_____2. I can recognize what makes me uncomfortable with differences that exist between myself and others in terms of race, ethnicity, and culture.

_____3. I am aware and have specific knowledge about my own racial and cultural heritage and how it personally affects my biases.

_____4. I am aware of and understand about how oppression, racism, discrimination, and stereotyping affect me personally and in my work.

_____5. I am aware of who I am, how I appear, and how I communicate; and how all of this may socially influence others.

_____6. I am aware of my negative and positive emotional reactions toward other racial and ethnic groups that may make it hard for me to work with them.

_____7. I have specific knowledge and information about the cultural groups I interact with. I am aware of the life experiences, cultural heritage, and historical background of my culturally different friends.

_____8. I count among my friends people who are culturally different from me.

Figure 6.4

Source: Adapted from "Operationalization of the Multicultural Counseling Competencies," by P. Arrendondo, R. Toporek, S. Brown, J. Jones, D. C. Locke, J. Sanchez, & H. Stadler, 1996, *Journal of Multicultural Counseling and Development, 24.* Alexandria, VA: American Counseling Association. Used with permission.

What this illustrates is that although various models exist, they are often complements to each other. Your challenge as a practitioner is to borrow liberally from these national models in order to use the language that will help students "get their needs met."

In this section, we provide an example of the development of a lesson plan, as we explain the steps, before asking you to develop your own. The steps we follow with our example, however, are the same steps you will follow in developing your lesson plan.

Our example is based on the assumption that a top priority is: *Students need to understand and appreciate their own diversity and that of others.*

1. Transform the needs statement to a student outcome statement. For example: *Students will understand and appreciate their own diversity and that of others.*

2. Determine the appropriate standard (using one or more of the national or state models or the learner outcomes that you have developed). As we stated in our "apples and apples" example, you have many choices.

3. Determine where this learning outcome will be taught. For example: *Middle/junior high school integrated arts class*

4. Write a task statement. For example: *Students will create a series of murals depicting the cultural diversity in the classroom.*

5. Develop the lesson plan, including the materials you will need, the procedure to follow, and any follow-up activities. For example:

Materials:

Large rolls of newsprint (obtainable at the local newspaper office as end rolls)
Colored markers
Miscellaneous drawing instruments
A large space in which to work

Procedure:

1. Administer the multicultural counseling competencies student pretest (Figure 6.4). Discuss the implications of some of the items that students identify.
2. As a homework assignment, ask the students to have a conversation with their parents or guardians about the celebration of a special event in their family when they (the students) were preteens. As a part of this assignment, ask them to list the parts of this event that might be specific to their heritage. Examples might include (a) visiting an aging aunt in a retirement community, (b) the marriage of a relative, or (c) celebrating a special holiday.
3. Divide the class into groups of five. (We suggest that you use a count-off method in the hopes that the groups will be heterogeneously organized.)
4. Ask the students to share their lists within the groups.
5. Ask the groups to organize how they will depict the activities on newsprint in the form of a mural. Emphasize that each group member needs to contribute and that we are looking for teamwork and creativity, and not artistic perfection. Give each group plenty of time to create a mural with which they will be pleased.
6. Have each group display their mural and describe it to the class.
7. Post the murals for others to see and for the class to reflect on.

Follow-up Activities:

Ask students to write about what they learned about the diversity of this class.
Ask students to bring food from home that represents their family's cultural heritage, for example, pumpkin muffins, blintzes, baklava, or beignés. Invite parents to participate.

Note: If this is a truly "integrated arts" class, several disciplines will be involved—for example, social studies, art, and English.

Figure 6.5 illustrates the lesson plan that has been developed using the previous steps and examples. Using these steps and our example as a guide, you will now develop your own lesson plan. We have provided a blank lesson form in Figure 6.6 on which you can practice.

Activity 6.1   The Lesson Plan

Using any student outcome that your group developed in Activity 5.7, create a complete lesson plan. Share your lesson plan ideas with other groups.

Summary

In this chapter, you have had an opportunity to begin to build a curriculum that fits the identified needs of your school and community. Not only have we asked you to consider writing your own curriculum, we also have given you an example that will challenge you to consider new dimensions of diversity. Figure 6.7 lists some curricula that we have found to be useful when developing our own.

Suggested outline for curriculum activity: Lesson plan

Outcome Statement:

Students will understand and appreciate their own diversity and that of others.

Activity Title:

Diversity mural

Grade Level: Middle/junior high school and integrated arts class

Time Allotted: 110 minutes

Task: Students will create a series of murals depicting the cultural diversity in the classroom.

Materials: Large rolls of newsprint (obtainable at the local newspaper office as end rolls)
Colored markers
Miscellaneous drawing instruments
A large space in which to work

Procedure:

1. Administer the multicultural counseling competencies student pretest (Figure 6.4). Discuss the implications of some of the items that students identify.

2. As a homework assignment, ask the students to have a conversation with their parents or guardians about the celebration of a special event in their family when they, the students, were preteens. As a part of this assignment, ask them to list the parts of this event that might be specific to their heritage. Examples might include (a) visiting an aging aunt in a retirement community, (b) the marriage of a relative, or (c) celebrating a special holiday.

3. Divide the class into groups of five.

4. Ask them to share their lists within the groups.

5. Ask the groups to organize how they will depict the activities on the newsprint in the form of a mural. Emphasize that each group member needs to contribute and that we are looking for teamwork and creativity, and not artistic perfection. Give each group plenty of time to create the mural.

6. Have each group display their mural and describe it to the class.

7. Post the murals for others to see and for the class to reflect on.

Follow-up Activities:

Ask students to write about what they learned about the diversity of this class.

Ask students to bring food from home that represents their family's cultural heritage, for example, pumpkin muffins, blintzes, baklava, or biegnés.

Figure 6.5

Outline for curriculum activity: Lesson plan

Outcome Statement: **Activity Title:**

Grade Level: **Time Allotted:**

Task:

Materials:

Procedure:

Follow-up Activities:

Figure 6.6

Elementary

Career-O-Rom-A, next generation career series—on CD. (1997). Itasca, IL: Wintergreen Orchard House/Riverside Publishing/Houghton-Mifflin. Call (800) 323-9540 for a catalog.

Center on Education and Work. (1995). *Developmental guidance: Classroom and small group activity guides [E].* Madison, WI: Author. (800) 446-0399.

Dream catchers. (1993). Indianapolis, IN: Jist Publications. Author: (800) 648-5478.

Parramore, B. M., Hopke, W. E., & Drier, Harry N. (1998). *Children's dictionary of occupations.* Bloomington, IL: Meridian Educational Corporation. (800) 727-5507.

Rogala, J. A., Lambert, R., & Verhage, K. (1992). *Developmental guidance classroom activities for use with the national career development guidelines* (Grades 4–6). Madison, WI: Center on Education and Work, University of Wisconsin-Madison. (800) 446-0399.

VanZandt, Z., & Buchan, B. A. (1998). *Lessons for life: Vol. 1. Elementary grades.* Des Moines, IA: Prentice-Hall. (800) 288-4745.

Middle/High School

Career finder plus—on CD (1998). Itasca, IL: Wintergreen Orchard House/Riverside Publishing/Houghton-Mifflin. Call (800) 323-9540 for a catalog.

Center on Education and Work. (1995). *Developmental guidance: Classroom and small group activity guides [M, H].* Madison, WI: Author. (800) 446-0399.

Norden, T., & Wysong, N. (Eds.). (1993). *Focus on your future: A career planning curriculum for teens.* Module I: Self-knowledge. Madison, WI: Center on Education and Work, University of Wisconsin-Madison. (800) 446-0399.

Oregon Occupational Information Coordinating Committee. (1989). *Schoolwork, lifework: Integrating career information into high school career development programs.* Salem, OR: Oregon Occupational Information Coordinating Committee.

VanZandt, Z., & Buchan, B. A. (1998). *Lessons for life: Vol. 2. Secondary Grades.* Des Moines, IA: Prentice-Hall. (800) 288-4745.

Figure 6.7 Curriculum resources

References

Arredondo, P., Toporek, R., Brown, S., Jones, J., Locke, D. C., Sanchez, J., & Stadler, H. (1996). Operationalization of the multicultural counseling competencies. *Journal of Multicultural Counseling and Development, 24.* Alexandria, VA: American Counseling Association.

Carr, J. V., Brook, C. A., Hayslip, J. B., Williams, F., & Zwolinski, M. (1997). *A manual for a comprehensive career guidance and counseling program.* Derry, NH: New Hampshire Comprehensive Guidance and Counseling Program, Inc.

Reflections on Chapter 6

1. What area of curriculum development do you still need to work on?

2. What curriculum resources do you already have that may fit your needs?

3. What are some of the difficulties in developing curriculum activities in a group?

4. What are some of the advantages in developing curriculum activities in a group?

5. Who could serve as your role model for doing classroom guidance? What would you learn from that person or those persons?

6. Notes:

# Chapter 7
Assigning Responsibilities

Who does what? In the first six chapters of this handbook, you have determined what needs to be done to accomplish a comprehensive, developmental school guidance and counseling program. As a team, you have completed a needs assessment and determined those elements within the program that take priority over others. In Chapter 7, you will describe the human and material resources available to you to make your program work.

If you have developed a time line that includes all the activities that need to be done, then you know you must include other people in the implementation. In Chapter 2, we described a collaborative approach to building an ideal school counseling program. By empowering others, we create broad ownership of the program. Each person involved has the capacity to challenge the status quo and give the program renewed energy. Involving people in developing the program will make them even more committed to its implementation, and involving as many as possible will help to ensure a broad base of support.

Be sure to include programs that are already being carried out in your school, such as peer-helper or teacher-advisor programs. The personnel who are conducting existing successful programs are valuable resources to you.

Now it is time to assign tasks and responsibilities to personnel and organizations—responsibilities that will get the job done. If, as a school counseling team, you have conducted a time and task analysis, you have determined the elements within your program that must be done by counselors and also the tasks that can be done by others. This is a critical point. For example, suppose someone needs to convene a committee meeting. Who is the best person to set up this meeting—the head counselor, the principal, or the school counseling department's secretary? As another example, say the team has determined that an advisory committee should be assembled. Who should draft the letter that invites business, industry, and community leaders to join this committee? Who should sign the letter?

PREPARING TO DELIVER YOUR PROGRAM

Borders and Drury (1992), in an exhaustive study that synthesized 30 years of empirical work and professional statements, concluded:

There is a general consensus among professionals concerning interventions that should be included in a comprehensive developmental school counseling program. . . . Both *direct* and indirect services are identified, and these are frequently categorized as *counseling* and *classroom guidance* (direct services), and *consultation* and *coordination* (indirect services). (pp. 490, 491)

In Chapter 4, we introduced the concept of "delivery systems," including a new "C," conducting activities, with classroom guidance curriculum emphasis. We are highlighting these delivery systems once again to help you think about possible alternatives for reaching your goals and meeting students' needs.

Counseling

Counseling, as a method of intervention, relates to the process for helping students overcome blocks to their personal and educational growth, and toward achieving maximum development of their potential. A counselor needs to determine when counseling is appropriate and when another delivery system may satisfy a client's needs just as well.

Within the delivery system, counselors need to make personal and professional choices related to theoretical approaches, ethical issues, and the limitations of the counseling intervention. A major program management consideration centers on the extent to which small group or individual counseling will be utilized.

Consultation

At times the counselor acts as an objective party, looking at a situation and suggesting developmental, preventive, remedial, and other helpful interventions without direct contact with the client whose needs are being addressed. Models of consultation exist to help counselors gain skills in this area. Meetings with teachers, parents, industrial managers, support personnel, and administrators often utilize the counselor's consultation skills.

Coordination

The successful counselor needs to be able to identify those tasks that can be done by another person, agency, or alternative means, and then provide the structure and input that will promote this intervention without the counselor's direct involvement. For example, referral systems, the facilitation of research studies, and career education infusion strategies demonstrate how counselors must be involved in organizing or facilitating such interventions, but also how careful coordination makes it possible for other personnel to implement these tasks as complements to the counseling program.

A counselor with good coordination skills may, at times, also enjoy the challenge of coordinating a major event or activity. Career days and guest lecture series illustrate how highly visible programs can reach many people through excellent coordination.

Conducting Activities

Many program activities just do not fit into the conventional three Cs; instead, they fall under a broad category making up the fourth C: *conducting activities*. Although such activities do require careful planning and coordination, the actual delivery of services may also require that the counselor be directly or indirectly involved in conducting the activity.

Classroom guidance is one broad category of conducting activities that may or may not be done directly by the counselor; in fact, it is most effectively done by the counselor and teacher working together. One example at the high school level is cooperation between the teacher and the counselor to help students with the essays and other forms they need to write to apply for college admission and/or to complete job applications. These skills could be taught in an English or social studies classroom; the completion of the essay could then earn class credit and accomplish the students' goal of being prepared for their next career step. The counselor would work with the teacher in preparing the lesson and might enter the classroom for a short period of time to present the concept; but the teacher would be the writing expert and would need to carry out the lesson in his or her own way.

Many public relations activities, such as writing news releases, fall under this category of conducting activities. Conducting orientation programs, leading group test interpretation sessions, training peer helpers, conducting financial aid nights, and similar programs also are classified under this rubric. Because the counselors are *actively* (or directly) involved with the clients in these activities, it is obvious that they are not consulting or coordinating. The indirect result of the activities, however, may be an increased involvement of teachers and other school staff members in the counseling delivery system.

Activity 7.1   Thinking Outside of the Box

Before we ask you to be involved in assigning responsibilities, we want you to begin to think outside of the box. We spent some time in Chapter 2 looking at functional and nonfunctional behavior in groups, but we need to remind you to continually look for (brainstorm) solutions that are innovative and may not at first seem to fit. A creativity exercise that we guarantee will work is to think outside of the box. We have borrowed this creativity exercise from Johnson and Johnson (1975), and we recommend that you stop and try it now. Try this individually, and then work in small groups to resolve how you can connect all nine dots in just four straight lines without lifting your writing utensil from the paper. You may want to use a pencil that has an eraser. The solution is at the end of this chapter, but no peeking.

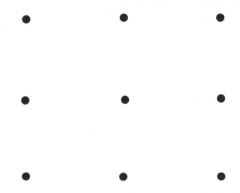

We have engaged you in an exercise that we hope will now motivate you to think creatively in deciding who will deliver various tasks for your school counseling program. Please keep the creative approach you used in this exercise in mind as you identify who will assign and carry out these tasks.

Activity 7.2 Appropriate Organizational Tasks

The following is a list of some tasks that must be done in an effective program. Beside each task, list the most appropriate person(s) or organization(s) to carry out that task. Please add some of your own tasks to this list.

- Master scheduling   *Principal* _____
- Four-year planning with students   *School counselor* _____
- Reception for parents for National
  School Counselor's Week
- Newsletter   _____
- Weekly local newspaper article   _____
- Classroom guidance lesson   _____
- Training of crisis team   _____
- Achievement tests administration   _____
- Achievement tests interpretation   _____
- Pupil evaluation team   _____
- Bulletin boards   _____
- _____   _____
- _____   _____
- _____   _____
- _____   _____

As a follow-up to this activity, review the list of tasks and the person(s) or organization(s) that you have listed as mainly responsible.

1. Which of these responsibilities do you see as "traditional" school counseling tasks?

2. If you have delegated these to others, how will you, or should you, monitor them so that you know they are being accomplished?

3. Is this the best use of staff expertise?

4. Is it possible to attach budget line items to the various program activities? If yes, which ones?

5. What is your time frame for changing from a service-oriented to a program-oriented delivery?

6. What other questions do you need to ask?

7. Looking at the preceding roles and responsibilities, describe your feelings about sharing power and authority with other professionals within and outside the school.

INSERVICE EDUCATION

Frequently, you and your counseling staff will determine that professionals within your school need to become more knowledgeable about a topic or a challenge before you can assign them a specific responsibility. Time that is set aside for schoolwide inservice education may be an opportunity for counselors to contribute to the inservice education of the teachers. For example, the counselors may have attended a conference where they learned about different learning styles. The counselors may believe that classroom teachers would benefit from an inservice day that focuses upon developing curriculum materials that meet the needs of different learning styles based upon new research and application. You may want to decide how your planning committee would set up an inservice training day so that teachers would attend and willingly participate. You need to set up the agenda for the day and determine how you would evaluate whether the teaching staff applied their new knowledge.

Activity 7.3 Exploring Inservice Education

In your group, explore the following questions related to inservice teacher/professional education.

1. Who in the group has conducted an inservice education program?

2. What is the best inservice program in which you have participated?

3. What makes a good inservice program?

4. What are the challenges to counselors conducting inservice programs?

We have talked about how difficult it is to create change. In working with this handbook, you may have noticed that change is a "constant" in school counseling programs. As a change agent in your school, think about how inservice education can be an integral part of the change process. Begin the same way you did with the curriculum development: look at your needs assessment data. If you have answered the questions in Activity 7.3, you can plan and deliver an inservice day in which faculty and staff will be excited to participate.

Certainly, you will need to attend to the details of the inservice program, but it is very important that you decide whether you will be the deliverer of or an active participant in the inservice activities you create. Do it yourself only if you are qualified to conduct such a program. If you call upon outside presenters or consultants, be sure that they are available for follow-up assistance.

Returning to our example of an inservice training on different learning styles, we need to keep in mind that teachers and administrative staff need to understand and appreciate their own teaching and learning styles, as well as those of their students, if they are to be fully engaged in the inservice program. Therefore, we have included an example of an inservice program for the Myers-Briggs Type Indicator, one of many learning styles inventories available, and we have written an agenda for an inservice training using this inventory (see Figure 7.1).

Myers-Briggs Type Indicator (MBTI) Introductory Workshop

Jo Hayslip, Career Transitions

June 19, 1999, Clover School District

Rationale: Educators who understand and appreciate their own teaching and learning styles and those of others are able to create an appropriate learning setting and accomplish more within that work setting.

Goals:

Participants will learn about and understand their own work styles and the work styles of others with whom they work (and live).

Participants will begin to use communication skills in their work and their personal lives based upon their understanding of the Myers-Briggs Type Indicator (MBTI).

Participants will develop a sense of their own teaching performance and be able to describe what is good about it and what needs to be improved.

Mini-lecture:

Why people take tests; how this "test" is different (Participants will have taken the MBTI but not scored it.)

Introduction to type: Participants will estimate their own type.

Participants will then score their MBTIs and translate their scores onto report forms. Discussion will follow.

Activity #1: Team Task

Career Transitions, a newly incorporated organization, has requested that your work group design a logo and/or a slogan for them. All that you know about them is that they provide workshops and seminars for persons who are making career decisions or career change decisions. Using your understanding and appreciation of type, design the best logo and/or slogan that your group then agrees to present to Career Transitions. Share and discuss.

Activity #2: Back at Work

Write on a card one new bit of information you learned about yourself that you are going to carry away from this workshop. Share with others in the group if you wish. Now write down how you are going to put this new bit of information into practice. Discuss.

Evaluation and Wrap-up

Figure 7.1 Example of an introductory workshop

Activity 7.4 Taking a Risk—Developing and Conducting an Inservice Program

Now we are going to ask you to take a significant risk by developing and coordinating an inservice education program for your faculty and administration. Using the curriculum development steps that you used in Chapter 6, develop and conduct an inservice day for faculty and administrative staff. We have provided a blank agenda (Figure 7.2) for you to use in planning your inservice program. If possible, conduct your inservice program off-site (outside of your typical work setting) to ensure that participants can stay focused on the task and not be distracted by phone calls and other emergencies. This is especially important for those staff in administration.

Name of Workshop _____

Presenter's Name _____

Date, Time, Place _____

Rationale:

Goals:

Mini-lecture:

Activity #1:

Activity #2:

Evaluation and Wrap-up

Figure 7.2 Workshop outline

Activity 7.5 Developing a Time Line

If all these activities seem to be overwhelming, remember that they do not have to be done all at once. It is important for everyone involved to understand what the procedures are and approximately when each step is expected to be completed. As much as possible, every member needs to be involved not only in planning the events but also in setting the time frames within which those events will take place. Figure 7.3 represents the time line that the New Hampshire Comprehensive Guidance and Counseling Program set for the first phase of its development. As the New Hampshire people worked with this time line, they discovered that they needed more than one year to accomplish all the tasks. We have provided a blank format in which the dates have been omitted (Figure 7.4) that you can use in developing your own time line.

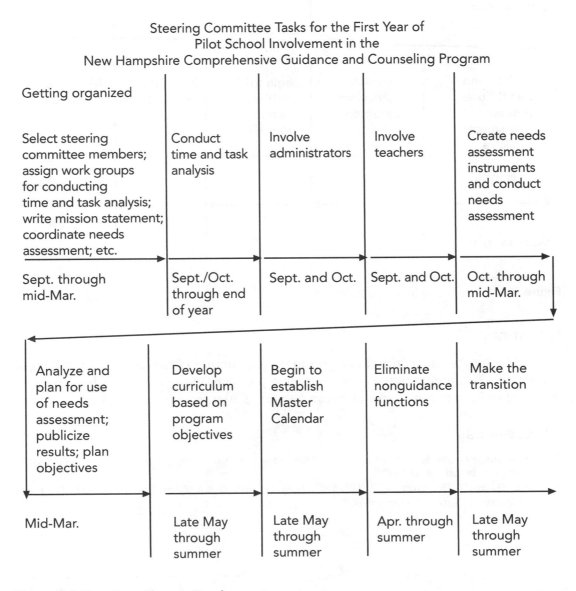

Steering Committee Tasks for the First Year of
Pilot School Involvement in the
New Hampshire Comprehensive Guidance and Counseling Program

Getting organized

Select steering committee members; assign work groups for conducting time and task analysis; write mission statement; coordinate needs assessment; etc.	Conduct time and task analysis	Involve administrators	Involve teachers	Create needs assessment instruments and conduct needs assessment
Sept. through mid-Mar.	Sept./Oct. through end of year	Sept. and Oct.	Sept. and Oct.	Oct. through mid-Mar.

Analyze and plan for use of needs assessment; publicize results; plan objectives	Develop curriculum based on program objectives	Begin to establish Master Calendar	Eliminate nonguidance functions	Make the transition
Mid-Mar.	Late May through summer	Late May through summer	Apr. through summer	Late May through summer

Figure 7.3 Time line—Phase 1: Development

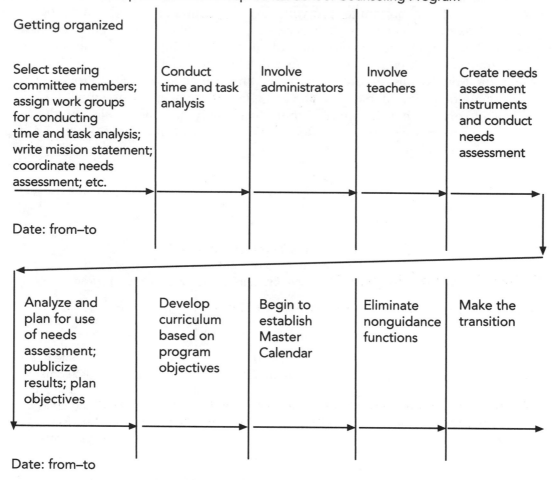

Figure 7.4 Time line—Phase 1: Development

Summary

In this chapter, we have introduced you to the importance of sharing responsibilities for delivering a comprehensive school counseling program. In addition, you have been introduced to further ways counselors can be part of an integrative curriculum.

References

Borders, D. L., & Drury, S. M. (1992). Comprehensive school counseling programs. *Journal of Counseling and Development, 70,* 487–498.

Johnson, D. W., & Johnson, F. P. (1975). *Joining together: Group theory and group skills* (2nd ed.). Englewood Cliffs, NJ: Prentice-Hall.

Solution to Problem in Activity 7.1

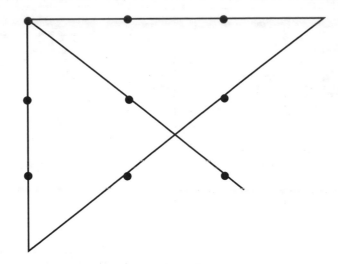

Reflections on Chapter 7

1. Describe what it was like to take a risk and promote an inservice program.

2. How easy (or difficult) is it to decide which tasks require a masters' degree in counseling and which tasks can be done by someone without that degree?

3. What is the most important thing you have learned about assigning responsibility within the school counseling program?

4. What questions do you have for yourself, your group members, or your facilitator?

5. Notes:

✠ Chapter 8

Organizing Program Support

You can have the best plan in the world, and it will sit on the shelf—unused and unappreciated—if you do not have the support of all the human and material resources needed to get the job done. In this chapter, we will explain some of those critical support systems.

PROGRAM POLICY STATEMENTS

To be an advocate for your program, you need to gather substantive policy statements that can lend clout to your arguments for a strong, comprehensive developmental school counseling program. By using carefully selected quotations from legislative mandates and endorsements from professional organizations or local school and district policies, you can add credibility to your planning efforts and gain important support.

Activity 8.1   Identifying Policy Support

Before you begin this activity, you may want to review Chapter 4, especially Figure 4.5, ASCA National Standards for School Counseling Programs; Figure 4.6, National Career Development Guidelines; and Figure 4.7, SCANS Competencies. Also refer to Appendix C, ASCA Position Statement, and Appendix E, ASCA Ethical Standards for School Counselors. These references, plus your own state standards and district-level policies and procedures, will help you to define the program support you need.

1. Poll the members of your cooperative learning group to see which people have access to local administrative offices, which people would be willing to contact local legislators, and which ones belong to professional educational organizations. Make sure each member of your group takes responsibility for communicating with one of these groups.
2. Each person is then given a homework assignment to search for written policy or endorsement statements that support the development of comprehensive developmental school counseling programs. Included could be statements supporting broad initiatives that address more global issues, such as programs to foster self-esteem.
3. Each person is responsible for finding direct quotations that can be shared with your group. The shorter and more concise they are, the more the statements will be read and understood.

4. Decide as a team whether certain quotations will be used in the presentation of your plan.

ADMINISTRATIVE SUPPORT

Without administrative support, it is unlikely that your program will flourish. The best possible scenario is to involve all administrators—principals, curriculum coordinators, and the superintendent—in the planning and implementation process. One way to accomplish this involvement is to create a form for the documents you produce that includes signed endorsements from these people. Even better, procure endorsements from the state principal, curriculum coordinator, and/or superintendent associations. When administrators take part in shaping the program, they will remain involved in developing the change process that moves the guidance offerings from a service-oriented, reactive process to a program-oriented, proactive initiative. They will see that school counseling has a program design and a budget similar to that of traditional disciplines, and they will help open the communication door to the community and the school board.

Activity 8.2   Involving Administration

Outline at least three actions that you will take to enlist and maintain the support of the administrators in your school district.

1.

2.

3.

ADVISORY COMMITTEE

Once your plan has been developed, you will need to enlist the support of some key people who can assist you with important decision making, the promotion of public understanding about program priorities, and future program initiatives. In most places, this committee is referred to as an advisory committee. This is a working committee that assumes important responsibilities in overseeing the school counseling program. This group is so significant that everything done until this point will succeed only if its members are solidly in support of your work.

Committee members should not be volunteers. The group is too important to the program for its composition to be left to chance. Choose committee members carefully, considering the perspectives and responsibilities you want each to bring to the group's makeup. The committee should be representative of different community constituencies; nonetheless, it should be as small and as manageable as possible. We will not tell you whom you should have on your advisory committee, except for one person: an administrator. An informed, supportive, and well-respected administrator can provide tremendous leverage for promoting change and enlisting cooperation. An administrator with K–12 responsibility can be very effective in helping counselors and those who are not counselors to maintain a K–12 perspective and to see the community implications for the committee's actions.

Some districts choose to use the committee that created their school counseling program as their advisory committee. Others use a group of proven veterans as their planning team, then open up membership to the advisory committee to new members who have expressed an interest in being more involved.

In convening the first meeting of the advisory committee (and probably each succeeding meeting as well, except in unusual circumstances), the head counselor (director of the school counseling program) should take an active leadership role. This means that the counselor should generate meeting announcements and agendas, facilitate the meetings, and be responsible for all written materials that flow out of the meetings. The counselor may choose to include the guidance secretary for taking minutes or to delegate responsibilities after the first meeting; either choice makes excellent use of personnel. Try to limit meetings to one hour (although this is not always possible, especially if the advisory committee is reviewing a significant document like the guidance curriculum). If you have short meetings with tight agendas, and every member leaves with a task to complete and report on at the next meeting, you should have excellent attendance.

Most people do not want to come to a meeting just to listen to someone talk about a program or to rubber-stamp something that has already been completed. Long before the first meeting, you should generate a list of items to which you would like your advisory committee members to attend. You may want to distribute this list during the first meeting so that people have a sense of purpose and role expectations are clear. The list may include some of the following:

1. Review printed materials about the school counseling program.
2. Discuss feedback from needs assessments.
3. Communicate information about guidance program priorities and services to other members of the community.
4. Present the perspective of the constituent group you represent.
5. Participate in National School Counseling Week activities.
6. Offer suggestions and advice about program offerings.
7. _____
8. _____
9. _____
10. _____

The list is not exhaustive by any means. It merely shows the types of assignments that can be given to advisory, steering, or planning committee members so they see the important roles they can play.

The job of managing the school counseling program ultimately falls on the shoulders of the counselor(s). You should not relinquish that responsibility to anyone else. You should always be open to (but not necessarily accepting of) any assistance that is offered. More important, however, you should feel confident that you have the knowledge and skills to use the information that you have gathered to establish appropriate priorities for your programs, to educate the public about program priorities, and then to create accountable programs.

RESOURCE AUDITS

Programs that can demonstrate they are making maximum use of existing resources are in a better position to request new or additional resources. You should conduct a resource audit to clarify what additional personnel, materials, equipment, and services will be needed to address the program goals that have been articulated.

Activity 8.3 Identifying Resources

1. What courses, programs, or teachers are already teaching the desired student learning outcomes? How successful are they? Are the students attaining the learning outcomes, and if so, to what degree? Begin your list here. We suggest that you may eventually need a grid or chart for this activity.

2. What additional human and material resources are needed for students to attain the desired learning outcomes? For example, are the members of the community willing to allow students to "shadow" workers in their businesses or industries? Are there enough Occupational Outlook Handbooks in the school counseling program area or library? Are the computerized college- and career-finding programs up-to-date? Begin your list here. We also suggest that you may need to develop a grid or chart for this activity, as well.

DEVELOPING YOUR BUDGET

You must establish an adequate budget that reflects the resource needs of the school counseling program. Keep in mind that the school counseling program budget needs to be separate from the testing budget, just as counselors should also be separated from the duty of coordinating testing in most situations. As the school counseling program in your district becomes an established program, your budget will take its place in the annual planning, like other school programs.

Activity 8.4 Designing the Budget

In your group, design a budget. Exclude salaries, fringe benefits, and schoolwide testing; these items are outside the school counseling program area and are usually located in the superintendent's budget or in the town or city report. Your budget should reflect the resources you need to provide a comprehensive developmental school counseling program to all the students in your district. One method might be to organize your budget to match the basic components of your program: guidance curriculum, individual planning, responsive services, and system support or program management. We have started your list; see how many more entries you can add.

Guidance Curriculum

Film/video rentals or purchases	$500.00
Primary grade curriculum/training	$400.00
AIDS education program	$1,000.00

Individual Planning

Career information system	$2,000.00
College information system	$1,000.00

Responsive Services

Inservice training: How to work with parents	$300.00

System Support

Postage and mailing for needs assessment	$400.00

Remember to include staff development funds to allow members of the counseling staff to keep their own competencies current.

GRANT WRITING

Writing grants has become a way of life for some school counseling programs. Many entitlement grants are available to schools to augment existing programs. Examples of such entitlement grants are (1) Drug-free Schools Program, for which each school/district must complete an annual application process; and (2) programs for special needs students, usually provided on a formula basis. Generally, there are strict guidelines that the school must follow, such as providing in-kind funding or space, or promising to continue the project after the funding runs out. Also, grants are offered for very specific purposes. Donors seldom simply hand out money for the recipients to use as they choose.

To establish and maintain "grantspersonship" at any level, one individual should be designated as directly responsible for obtaining the grant information and, once the grant has been won, for carrying out the procedures within the grant. Some systems have office personnel whose only purpose is researching, writing applications for, and monitoring grants. Other systems rely on professionals within the different disciplines to determine the importance of the grant and then to write the proposal and carry out the grant, if awarded.

Include in your grant-writing efforts small special funding requests that involve local, regional, and special projects. Often, local community groups and service organizations are looking for opportunities to invest time, funds, and energy into the student population. Projects that cost as little as $50 or $100 or up to $1,000 can provide your program with needed resources *and* promote positive linkages with your community.

Before you request funding, you must decide how you are going to use the funds. Then you need to match your purpose to the person or organization from whom you are requesting the funding. For example, your school library may need an updated set of occupational outlook materials. You might consider writing a request to a local employer or to the regional office of the Department of Education and Training (DET). Where else might you look?

Activity 8.5 Identifying Funding Sources

To identify possible grant sources, remember where you identified some gaps in resource materials. Brainstorm some needs, possible sources, and methods for contacting these resources. We have given you a couple of examples to get you started.

Need	Possible Source	Approach	Committee Contact
1. Occupational outlook materials	Dep't of Employment & Training	Letter/phone	Business teacher
2. Computer software program	Local bank	Personal contact	Computer teacher
3.			
4.			
5.			
6.			
7.			
8.			
9.			
10.			

In addition to these sources, you might consider using references that are directly targeted for proposal writing. Two that we have identified are *Getting Funded: A Complete Guide to Proposal Writing* (Hall, 1988) and *How to Fund Your Career Guidance Program* (Durgin & Drier, 1991). These and other sources indicate that you do not have to be an expert grant-writer to win grants.

Both authors of this handbook have written proposals and received funding for a number of grants—some for as little as $200, and others as large as $100,000. The key to receiving grant money is to follow the guidelines printed in the request for proposal (RFP)—the document from the funding source that announces the grant's availability and specifies the requirements for those seeking to qualify for the funds. Also, you need to ask yourself, "Do I have the expertise not only to write the grant but also to follow through with the implementation if I win the funding?"

Once you have read the grant application thoroughly and have determined that you will write it, heed the following suggestions as you write your proposal:

1. Write clearly and specifically; do not use jargon.
2. Be sure there is a logical theme running throughout your proposal and that all parts of the proposal directly relate to the grant's purpose.
3. Give equal attention to each section of the narrative part of the proposal.
4. Keep the proposal within the specified number of pages.
5. Write out the budget explanation, showing the categories you would use and the amount to be allocated to each.
6. Write objectives at the outcome level.
7. Write objectives in measurable terms.
8. Make sure your evaluation strategies are directly related to objectives and that they represent good evaluation design criteria.
9. Review the guidelines to ensure that your proposal satisfies all of them.
10. Be sure to follow the mailing instructions.

Once you have written your proposal, ask one or two people who have not been involved in the writing to critique it. Be sure to give them the proposal criteria. Ask them to pretend they are sitting in a windowless room at the U.S. Department of Education in Washington, D.C., and that this is the fiftieth proposal they have read. Take their critique seriously, make the necessary changes, and then send your grant application to the proper address. Good luck!

Summary

In this chapter, we have emphasized the importance of support from peers, subordinates, and superordinates. In order for your comprehensive developmental school counseling program to flourish, you must have everyone moving with you in the same direction. Careful inclusion of all factions along the way should be proving, at this point in your planning, that the change from a reactive service to a proactive program is happening or is about to happen.

References

Durgin, R., & Drier, H. (1991). *How to fund your career guidance program.* Omro, WI: COIN.
Hall, M. (1988). *Getting funded: A complete guide to proposal writing.* Portland, OR: Continuing Education Publications.

Reflections on Chapter 8

1. Of all of the people with whom you must work to garner support for your program, which one presents the greatest challenge? Why?

2. What can you do about it?

3. What made budget development doable in that activity in this chapter?

4. What questions do you have for yourself, your group members, or your facilitator?

5. Notes:

◈ Chapter 9

Developing Public Awareness and Support

In Chapter 1, we mentioned that public awareness and support (PAS) is such an important topic that we devote an entire chapter to it. We are convinced, however, that even a whole chapter will not do justice to the significance of this aspect of your total program. The image of school counseling programs and the image of the profession itself is dependent on the public's perception of what we do and whether we appear to be successful in doing it. The responsibility for building and maintaining the image of the profession of counseling rests as much with the individual counselor as it does with the professional organizations. No matter how you feel about it, you *will* have a public awareness and support program, whether it is intentional or not. Intentional public awareness just makes a lot more sense.

CREATING AN INVITING ATMOSPHERE

You need to consider the influence of the media to appreciate the role that public awareness and support play in our lives. Can any of us say that we are not persuaded, on occasion, to buy something because of how it is presented on television or the clever message describing it on the radio or in the newspaper? We are not suggesting that school counseling programs develop major campaigns just for the purpose of improving their image. A very pointed message from the public awareness literature is that public relations cannot disguise an inadequate program. We advocate a "truth in advertising" perspective that attempts to inform the public, accurately and thoroughly, about what they might realistically expect from the school counseling program.

Activity 9.1 The Medium Is the Message

1. In a small group, discuss the ways media influence you in making decisions in your daily lives. Areas for consideration might be:

   clothes buying
   hobbies and toys
   grocery shopping

health and medicine
political campaigns
sports and fitness
entertainment
service providers

Just in case members of your group maintain they are never influenced by the media, discuss how "the masses" are influenced by television, radio, and print media.

2. What are the implications for school counseling programs? Generate a list of these implications.

3. Develop a rationale for the public awareness efforts of your school counseling program.

Each of the authors has been responsible for the development of public awareness resources. Zark developed the *School Counselor's Resource Kit,* an annual public relations effort of the American School Counselor Association (ASCA), and Jo has taken a major role in promoting the *Public Awareness Ideas and Strategies for Professional Counselors,* a document published annually by the American Counseling Association. The challenge of putting such resources together is not unlike the challenge confronting each school counseling program: What do we emphasize, and what do we omit—and what is the best way to present ourselves? We cannot dismiss such a major challenge with the promise that we will work it out if we find the time! We need a plan. Public awareness strategies must be a major component of the overall management plan that we develop for our school counseling program.

PUBLIC AWARENESS CATEGORIES

One of the insights gained from working on the *School Counselor's Resource Kit* was the importance of categorizing the various ways that counselors can be responsive to the need for public awareness. There are so many things counselors can do related to public awareness that if we gave you a cumulative list of all the ideas we have gathered over the years, you might be overwhelmed. We want you to be excited about conducting public awareness activities, not overwhelmed! By putting the various possibilities into six broad categories, the task seems to be more manageable and more integrated with other tasks that the counselors must do.

Activities: Organizing Public Awareness Strategies

For each of the following categories—accountability, professional services, professionalism, publicity, student activities and events, and visual displays—we have provided you with one or two public awareness strategies that typify that category. Working in dyads or triads, brainstorm strategies for one of the six categories. Each small group should assume responsibility for a different category. Be prepared to present your work to the large group. We want you to use the creativity and resourcefulness of your small groups to generate other possibilities, since we believe that if you come up with the ideas, you will have more ownership and motivation to use them. Do not feel limited by the space provided. List all the good ideas that you can think of on a separate sheet of paper if necessary.

Activity 9.2   Public Awareness Through Accountability

Because of your own sense of commitment to the ideals of accountability, as described in Chapter 1, you determine which activities will be most responsive to the demands of those who use and evaluate your program.

1. Submit an annual report to the school board, demonstrating how well you have addressed the goals of your comprehensive plan.
2. Meet regularly with building administrators.

3. _____
    _____
4. _____
    _____
5. _____
    _____

Activity 9.3   Public Awareness Through Professional Service

There are many opportunities both within the school and in the community to be involved in activities that contribute to human development. Your visibility, commitment, and expertise will almost always be appreciated. More important, the public will see the linkages between the mission of the school counseling program and the goals and activities of various groups who have the students' best interests in mind.

1. Serve on the advisory committee of a local community service organization.
2. Be an advisor for a school club.

3. _____
    _____
4. _____
    _____
5. _____
    _____

Activity 9.4 Public Awareness Through Professionalism

Professionalism is the ingredient that helps professional counselors take the basic foundation provided by their educational training and build on it, so that they continue to grow professionally and assume responsibility for promoting and maintaining the image of the profession (VanZandt, 1990).

1. Present a workshop at a state counseling conference.
2. Be a model of mental and physical wellness.

3. _____

   _____

4. _____

   _____

5. _____

   _____

Activity 9.5 Public Awareness Through Publicity

Communicating through the media can help to inform, educate, and enlighten the public. The messages and images that are created through the media can have a lasting effect on the public's perception of our school counseling programs.

1. Regularly send out a school counseling program newsletter.
2. Share program activities through the local cable TV station.

3. _____

   _____

4. _____

   _____

5. _____

   _____

Activity 9.6 Public Awareness Through Student Activities and Events

There are many special programs and group activities that may require some organization and coordination on the counselor's part, but the dividends are great in terms of students' levels of investment and depth of involvement.

1. Celebrate National School Counseling Week (always the first full week of February).
2. Develop a Step-Up Day for students who will be entering or leaving the school the following year.

3. _____

   _____

4. _____

   _____

5. _____

   _____

Activity 9.7   Public Awareness Through Visual Displays

By aesthetically displaying information and messages in conspicuous places, we can draw people's attention to key elements of our school counseling program.

1. Develop attractive bulletin boards that focus on the themes from the guidance curriculum.
2. Wear lapel pins with counseling messages on them.
3. _____
   _____
4. _____
   _____
5. _____
   _____

Each time you develop a strategy or activity, write down the answers to the following questions:

1. When will I begin? (Hint: One good answer is *now*!)

2. With whom do I need to meet? (colleagues, teachers, principal, and so on. Use specific names.)

3. Where do I begin? (here, in a staff meeting, and so on)

4. How do I begin? (lead, assist, facilitate, and so on)

5. How will I know when the task is completed? (outcome or competency statement)

It is obvious from these activities that there are many opportunities to portray counselors and their programs in an accurate and positive light. The possibilities for public awareness and support are as extensive as the imaginations of those who take the time to generate a list of strategies, and to follow through by carrying out the strategies. This is why public awareness becomes an ideal way to involve your planning or advisory committee. Some advisory committees will want to be involved in the actual implementation of the activities or strategies; others will only want to take part in the brainstorming or decision making. Either way, the advisory committee needs to be kept informed of the progress of the implementation. Program leaders need to assess the committee members' level of commitment to this task to determine their desired involvement and to delegate responsibilities.

Activity 9.8   Plan of Action

As a final activity, we want you to create an annual public awareness and support plan of action (POA). From the numerous possibilities, we want your group to choose at least one initiative for each month of the school year. (Taking on one a month seems to be more realistic than trying to do everything on the lists that were generated—and will make you feel good about your accomplishments.)

As you plan your activity, keep in mind that you also will need to evaluate your progress, and make notes that will help you improve future efforts. We have filled in November in Figure 9.1 to illustrate this point. Complete the lefthand column in Figure 9.1. for the remaining months. When you have completed this chart, on a separate sheet of paper, write action steps you will need to take to fulfill each activity.

After completing this plan of action, discuss in your group whether the plan satisfies all the goals you have set for your team in promoting an accurate and positive image of your school counseling program. What changes might you consider?

As a final note, we want to remind you that public awareness is a critical part of program support and a significant part of program management. As with other management tasks, we must set aside time to make sure these tasks receive the needed attention. It is a matter of establishing public awareness and support as a priority.

NOTES FROM THE INTERNET*

Since the first edition of this book was published, the Internet has opened a number of dialogues or listservs in which members generously share their successful activities. For example, on the International Counseling Network listserv, there has been a continuing discussion about creating public awareness and support for school counseling programs. To sign on, send the message "subscribe ICN" to ICN@listserv.utk.edu. Russell Sabella, the listserv owner, will welcome you and encourage your participation.

Recently, Dr. Sabella began a dialogue by stating: "Because administrators and school boards do not know what we do, our jobs tend to be behind the scenes and hard to quantify. They will sacrifice where there is a perceived position not necessary."

Some of Dr. Sabella's own activities include:

1. Guest lecturing about comprehensive developmental guidance and counseling in courses that prepare future principals, especially about how to support such programs
2. Focusing on administrator publications and similar readerships for journal publishing
3. Making a part of school counselor training, methods for educating stakeholders about the purpose, value, and ways to support guidance and counseling. For instance, students in Dr. Sabella's Consulting with Teachers and Parents course all develop multimedia presentations, with accompanying learning activities, for

---

* Used with permission of Russell A. Sabella

Progress Chart

September	
Activity	Progress Comments

October	
Activity	Progress Comments

November	
Activity: Participate in Poster Contest and Poetry Contest as part of National Career Development Month.	Progress: Lots of participation in poster contest. Need to get Language Arts teachers excited about Poetry Contest. Comments: Next year, meet with all departments to determine interest.

December	
Activity	Progress Comments

Figure 9.1

January	
Activity	Progress
	Comments

February	
Activity	Progress
	Comments

March	
Activity	Progress
	Comments

April	
Activity	Progress
	Comments

Figure 9.1 Continued

May	
Activity	Progress
	Comments

June	
Activity	Progress
	Comments

July	
Activity	Progress
	Comments

August	
Activity	Progress
	Comments

Figure 9.1 Continued

helping site-based decision-making committees have better information about how to support school counseling

4. Working with state counseling associations and local districts in his area

Dr. Sabella asks, "How about members of the ICN share other ideas and ways to do this kind of thing. No matter how obvious, sometimes we just need to be reminded or recharged. . . ." Some replies that he has received, which may reflect some ideas that you have already written in your plan, include:

1. Present at parent-teacher organization meetings. Be the program.
2. Present at school board meetings. This needs to be built into your planning documents.
3. Convene a meeting of all 9th-grade parents. Explain the four-year process and its articulation with the K–12 format. Have the parents tell you how their children, and their children's younger siblings, will benefit from this program.
4. Invite parents to see the software or computer programs you use.
5. Present your program at the next faculty meeting. Facilitate a discussion that will help the faculty to tell you ways to make your program a success.

Summary

In this chapter, we have given you some strategies to help you "blow your own horn." It is important to do this loud and clear so that everyone knows what is going on. We have found that no one really likes surprises, and the more the public is informed, the more likely they are to "get on the bandwagon."

References

American Counseling Association. (1999). *Public awareness ideas and strategies for professional counselors.* Alexandria VA: Author.

American School Counselor Association. (1999). *School counselor's resource kit.* Alexandria VA: Author.

Sabella, Russell. ICN@listserv.utk.edu

VanZandt, C. E. (1990). Professionalism: A matter of personal initiative. *Journal of Counseling and Development, 68,* 243–245.

Reflections on Chapter 9

1. What are some public awareness activities that you have already been doing?

2. What are some public awareness activities that you need to do?

3. What is your level of commitment to public awareness and support in a comprehensive developmental school counseling model?

4. What questions do you have for yourself, your group members, or your group facilitator?

5. Notes:

Chapter 10

Establishing Program Leadership and Supervision

Just as there are styles of learning, there are styles of leadership. Each organization needs to utilize the leadership potential within all of its members. Encouraging individuals within the organization to utilize their leadership skills for different tasks makes it possible to complete work that one designated or elected leader could not accomplish alone. Often, the designated leader assumes all of the responsibility for all of the tasks and is not able to delegate work to colleagues. Or a designated leader might choose to delegate all of the tasks, and not set a work example for colleagues.

LEADERSHIP STYLES

There are great differences in leadership styles that need to be understood and honored. We recognize, for example, that identifying the school counseling program coordinator is a top priority. As program coordinators are identified (and perhaps information about their personality styles are shared), their leadership styles need to be described. A great deal of time and energy can be saved if everyone understands and agrees to work with an identifiable leadership style.

Activity 10.1   Identifying Leadership Styles

Two people who have studied leadership styles, Hersey and Blanchard (1992), have identified leadership styles in four different domains or quadrants. If possible, before you go any further in this chapter, complete and score a leadership styles instrument—for example, Hersey and Blanchard's *Leadership Effectiveness and Adaptability Description (LEAD)*— or use the Leadership Styles Inventory in this chapter (Figure 10.1).

Now ask yourself and your classmates these questions.

1. Do your results fit with your idea of your leadership style?
2. For what purposes and in what situations will your leadership style work best? Where will it work least well?

LEADERSHIP STYLES

Directions: For each item below, choose the letter of the response that most closely describes how you act in your role as supervisor. Base your choice on how you actually act, not how you think you should respond.

C 1. Rules and Regulations

    a. Insist that your subordinates follow the rules and regulations without exception.

    b. Allow your subordinates to do what they think is "right."

    c. Listen to your subordinates' explanation of exceptions to the rules and regulations and take these explanations into consideration.

b 2. Problem Solving

    a. Wait for your subordinates to discover the problem and find their own solutions.

    b. Solicit new ideas and solutions from your subordinates.

    c. Determine and implement new ideas and solutions as you deem appropriate.

C 3. Deadlines

    a. When approaching a deadline, require frequent updates from your subordinates.

    b. Allow your subordinates to complete their work as is convenient for them.

    c. Discuss the importance of meeting deadlines with your subordinates and solicit their cooperation.

b 4. Work Assignments

    a. Permit subordinates to decide their own work assignments without interference.

    b. Ask for volunteers for work assignments.

    c. Assume responsibility for assigning work tasks.

a 5. Interpersonal Relations

    a. Confine interactions with subordinates to work-related issues.

    b. Help your subordinates solve their personal problems.

    c. Avoid interactions with subordinates.

LEADERSHIP STYLES—SCORING

Directions: Circle the letter corresponding to your response for each item. Then, total the number of 1s, 2s, and 3s circled.

	1. a = 1	b = 3	c = 2
	2. a = 3	b = 2	c = 1
	3. a = 1	b = 3	c = 2
	4. a = 3	b = 2	c = 1
	5. a = 1	b = 2	c = 3
Totals	1	2	3
	1	4	4 9

Lower scores indicate a more Autocratic style of leadership (5–7).

Average scores indicate a more Democratic style of leadership (8–12).

Higher scores indicate a more Laissez-faire style of leadership (13–15).

Figure 10.1 Leadership styles inventory

Source: Developed by L. Painter and C. E. VanZandt, 1988, University of Southern Maine, Gorham.

3. Is there a relationship between your leadership style and your personality type as described by the MBTI or another personality assessment?

4. Is this style congruent with your perception of a guidance counselor?
5. Develop a profile of the leadership styles of the class.
6. Develop a matrix of the relationship of the personality instrument and the leadership style inventory results. What similarities do you perceive? What differences?

Just as there is no one ideal personality type, there is no one leadership style that is perfect for every challenge that a counselor meets in the everyday counseling situation. What is important is the ability to adapt one's style to fit key situations within the work environment.

Activity 10.2 Utilizing Leadership Style

As you are working within your task groups for the balance of this class, try to identify the leadership style that is being utilized at any given moment. On a given night, stop every five minutes to evaluate this, or evaluate it at times when you are stuck or when things are going smoothly. Try to do this consciously without interrupting the flow of your work.

Activity 10.3 Matching Leadership Styles to Group Functions

Refer back to the group roles activity in Chapter 2, Figure 2.1. Review the role functions that you first identified for your group. Are they still the same, or have they changed? For example, was the person who was the gatekeeper still performing that role? The person you have chosen as the director of guidance should facilitate this activity.

Activity 10.4 Developing Job Descriptions

Before beginning this activity, you may want to refer to Appendix A, ASCA Role Statement: The School Counselor; Appendix B, School Counselor Competencies; Appendix C, ASCA Position Statement: The School Counselor and Developmental Guidance; and Appendix D, The School Counselor and Comprehensive School Counseling Programs. Using Figure 10.2, review the job description of the Director of School Counseling Programs at Clover High School and (a) determine the leadership attributes that exist in the job description, (b) determine what other desired attributes need to be added to the job description, and (c) rewrite the job description to reflect the kind of leader your group desires.

The director of school counseling programs may be referred to under a number of titles. Figure 10.2 is a typical job description for the Director of School Counseling Programs at Clover School District. Ideally, the person in this position has experience at both the elementary and secondary levels *and* has the authority to supervise the K–12 program.

TITLE: Director of School Counseling Programs

LOCATION: Clover School District

REPORTS TO: Superintendent of Schools

PROFESSIONAL QUALIFICATIONS: Masters Degree in Counseling from an accredited program; 3 years of experience as a school counselor, preferably with experience at elementary and secondary levels; qualify for certification as a school counselor in this state; knowledge of services for accommodating the needs of all students; experience in the development, implementation, and evaluation of comprehensive guidance and counseling programs.

PERSONAL QUALIFICATIONS: Excellent verbal and written communication skills; evidence of leadership skills; committed to program accountability and public relations; value teamwork; committed to group and classroom guidance approaches; flexible about time and work commitments; highly motivated and enthusiastic.

JOB FUNCTIONS: The individual filling this position shall be responsible for:

1. Developing, coordinating, implementing, and evaluating a written K–12 school counseling program based on the State Comprehensive Guidance and Counseling Program Model

2. Directing school counseling programs and guidance services at the high school level to students identified in the following programs:

   a. vocational

   b. students with exceptionalities

   c. students at risk

   * Note: All other students will be assigned to other counselors in the school district

3. Conducting regular public relations activities for the department at all levels

4. Organizing and meeting with a K–12 school counseling program advisory committee at least three times annually

5. Establishing linkages and networks among the high school, junior high school, and elementary school counselors, and community agencies providing services to the identified students

6. Submitting an annual report to superiors, highlighting program goals, accomplishments, future needs, suggested changes, and areas of concern

Figure 10.2 Job description

MODELS OF SUPERVISION

The job description in Figure 10.2 is a perfect lead-in to our discussion of supervision. A good director of school counseling programs should be able to demonstrate competence in the areas of both leadership *and* supervision. Although the two entities are quite distinct, there is some overlap that synergistically helps mold a quality director of school counseling programs. A good leader will recognize and promote essential supervision practices. The good supervisor recognizes that effective leaders and role models may play significant parts in the professional development of a counselor. Furthermore, a good supervisor will nurture the leadership abilities of those he or she supervises, and a good leader will recognize that each counselor needs to develop to a point that he or she can eventually assume the role of supervisor. It is obvious that a reciprocal relationship and a developmental perspective provide a healthy framework in which both leadership and supervision can evolve.

Counselor supervisors typically play four major roles: counselor, consultant, evaluator, and educator. Simplistically, there are times when a supervisor may need to validate the feelings and needs of the counselor (supervisee), be able to discuss alternative interventions and facilitate decision making about a case, be able to assess areas of strength and weakness within the supervisee's skill repertoire, and be able to suggest educational resources and opportunities that "fill in the gaps" in a supervisee's training. There may be times when a supervisor will play all four roles within one supervision session.

A full discourse on the competencies that supervisors should possess is beyond the scope of this handbook. The purpose of exploring the topic here is quite different than that of the American Counseling Association in endorsing 11 core areas of knowledge, skills, personal traits, and recommended training activities for supervisors (Dye & Borders, 1990). As members of a school counseling team, you need to appreciate the importance of supervision for the overall efficient management of your program and for the development of your counseling skills as you assist others with their developmental needs. Supervision is usually divided into two broad categories, administrative supervision and counselor supervision, so it is important for school counselors to seek both kinds of supervision as they develop within the field.

CONCEPTUAL FRAMEWORK FOR SUPERVISION

Portions of the following material are taken liberally (with permission) from a position paper written by Carl Bucciantini (1999) for the Auburn, Maine, schools. It was developed as part of the three-course sequence in supervision offered within the Certificate of Advanced Study, University of Southern Maine, Gorham, Maine. For further information, please contact Carl Bucciantini at the Auburn schools. This proposal was designed to be specific to the Auburn School Department; but with minor adaptations, it can be applied to any school system that desires to provide this level of support to its counselors.

Supervision for school counselors is defined similarly to supervision in other mental health professions, though issues may vary.

> [Supervision is an] intervention provided by a more senior member of a profession to a more junior member or members of that same profession. This relationship is evaluative, extends over time, and has the simultaneous purposes of enhancing the professional functioning over the more junior person(s), monitoring the quality of professional services offered to the client(s) she, he, or they see(s). . . . (Bernard & Goodyear, 1998, p. 6)

Another similar definition of supervision was adopted by the Association of Counselor Education and Supervision (ACES) in 1969:

> Counselor supervision is performed by experienced, successful counselors (supervisors) who have been prepared in the methodology of supervision. It facilitates the counselor's personal and professional development, promotes counselor competencies, and promotes accountable counseling and guidance services and programs. It is the *purposeful* function of overseeing the work of counselor trainees or practicing counselors (supervisees) through a set of supervisory activities that includes consultation, counseling, training and instruction, and evaluation. (VanZandt, 1984, pp. 14–15)

Supervision takes place in a relational context; it is first and foremost a relationship between professionals. All supervisor approaches recognize the relational component of supervision, but with varying degrees of emphasis. Regardless of the view taken, however, the supervisor-supervisee relationship appears to be a necessary ingredient in the making, doing, and being of the supervisory process itself and seemingly facilitates or potentiates whatever takes place within that process.

Supervision, whether provided in a school or mental health setting, should be offered to counselors individually and in group settings. Individual supervision is probably still considered to be the cornerstone of professional development. Individual supervision affords both the supervisor and the supervisee the opportunity to explore in depth any presenting issues using a variety of interventions geared specifically to meeting the supervisee's needs.

Group supervision, as defined by Holloway and Johnston (1985), is

> the regular meeting of a group of supervisees with a designated supervisor, for the purpose of furthering their understanding of themselves as counselors, of the clients with whom they work, and/or of service delivery in general, and who are aided in this endeavor by their interaction with each other in the context of the group process. (p. 333)

School counselors are unique in the school system. Others in the school setting are free to discuss problems with children in the classrooms and to consult with teachers and administrators. Confidentiality guidelines apply only to school counselors. Further, the problems that school counselors routinely deal with are often very intense: suicidal ideation, abuse, running away, leaving school, pregnancy, and substance abuse, to name only a few. School counselors need a place to discuss these issues, to feel supported, and to grow without "burning out" from this very exciting and demanding job. School counselors deserve supervision (Fall, 1998).

The practical considerations to be examined in order to offer supervision to school counselors in the school district include:

- Assessing whether the counselors feel the need for support
- Determining the level of administrative support available
- Making sure all involved have a clear understanding of what supervision is and is not
- Determining whether to offer supervision for all counselors or just those who request it
- Creating a new staff position of counselor supervisor
- Providing the time for counselors to meet for individual and group supervision
- Making provision for the supervision of supervision

These practical considerations are crucial to the success of creating a position for a supervisor on staff. Without the support of all stakeholders, this proposal, no matter how well reasoned, is doomed to failure.

School counselors, by receiving supervision, experience the feeling of support, self-awareness, and professional growth that comes with introspection, questioning, and structure of supervision. The benefits to the school department are directly linked to the benefits of the individual. If the counseling staff is able to attend to its professional needs in an organized, effective, and predictable manner, then the entire organization wins. Or, to modify a mathematical maxim, in this case the whole is greater than the sum of its parts (synergy).

A final note about supervision competencies: Competencies are usually divided into three broad categories—knowledge, skills, and traits. The knowledge and skills are fairly easy to assess. Your counselor training program has probably used tests, projects, and observation checklists to determine your ability to perform in many areas. Traits, however, are considerably more difficult to measure. For example, you might believe that a supervisor should be "sensitive." Most would agree that sensitivity is an admirable trait in a counselor and in a supervisor, but we would also find it difficult to agree on one acceptable definition or on any observable indicators that objectify the concept of sensitivity. Many would also be concerned that counselors and supervisors could be too sensitive. Even though traits are subject to this dilemma of objectivity, the professionals who worked together to validate the supervision competencies through extensive research studies found that relationship factors were considered to be as important as technical skills in good supervision. One way to strengthen responses in this area was to clarify terms so that they have more specific relevance to the counseling field. Thus, instead of just using the term *sensitive*, one competency reads "is sensitive to the counselor's personal and professional needs" (Association for Counselor Education and Supervision, 1989, p. 9).

Activity 10.5 The Model Supervisor

In your groups, explore the competencies of good supervisors through the following tasks.

1. On a chalkboard or flipchart, create three columns with the headings:

   KNOWLEDGE   **SKILLS**   **TRAITS**

2. Have group members brainstorm competencies they believe a good counselor supervisor should possess. Have the group reach consensus regarding in which column the competency should be placed.
3. Again, through consensus, identify the three competencies in each category that seem to be most important. Put an asterisk next to each of these.
4. Discuss the challenges of being a top-notch supervisor.

Just as careful training, skill development, and dedication are needed to shape the competence of supervisors, those who are supervised must also assume responsibility for maximizing the supervision experience. Obviously, supervision is a process of communicating about skills, techniques, performance, and accountability. There must be two-way communication, or supervision is going to be useless. Therefore, we all need to examine how we receive, process, and use feedback to maximize our performance.

Activity 10.6 The Model Supervisee

Individually respond to each of the following questions; then, in your group, discuss the ideal supervisee. Record your findings on a flipchart or chalkboard.

1. What foundational knowledge and skills should a counselor bring to the supervision encounter?

2. What traits will assist the supervisee in taking full advantage of the opportunity provided by working with a person with more experience and training?

3. What should the supervisee look for in terms of program management supervision?

4. How can the supervisee assist the supervisor with counseling supervision?

Counselors as Leaders

Program leadership and supervision may seem far removed from the critical issues confronting a school counseling program; however, that kind of thinking can only spell trouble for everyone concerned. All counselors must see themselves as leaders. There are so many ways to be a leader that it is just a matter of deciding how you will assert your leadership and how you will contribute to the overall goals and activities of the school counseling program. In the same light, supervision must concern all counselors, from the neophyte counselor just entering the profession to the venerable helpers who are now working with the grandchildren of their first clients. The profession is too complex and profound to allow any member to rest on the credentials offered by the *minimum* standards rendered by a master's degree in school counseling. In the developmental continuum, we should always be trying to improve ourselves.

A good supervisor is a leader; however, a leader is not necessarily a good supervisor. But any quality school counseling program must have both good supervision and good leadership. Any time one member of the program's team fails to do his or her part in contributing to the "whole" in a well-run system, leaders and supervisors should recognize the problem and take steps to refocus the individual before the system breaks down. It is said that a chain is only as strong as its weakest link, and supervisors and leaders in a school counseling program should be working diligently to ensure that the weakest link is not weak at all.

CHALLENGES TO THE CHANGE AGENT

We have presented information about leadership and supervision, but we also need to talk about the counselor as change agent. Often counselors are the ones who clearly see the big picture because they work within the system but "outside of the box." The students have a different relationship with the counselor and count on the counselor to interpret their thoughts and feelings to the school and the community. In the final analysis, the counselor may see the need for change and must help make these changes within the system on behalf of the students. We need to be thoughtful and caring at the same time that we are becoming assertive advocates of change. As change agents, we need to ask the following questions.

Activity 10.7 Making Change

1. *Where does the power come from?* Are you perceived as a person with power, or do you need the support of those who have it?

2. *Do you have the skills to help others conceptualize the needed change?* Writing skills, utilizing the systems approach, creating management plans, speaking skills, and creating diagrams and models are all necessary skills. How can you obtain these skills, if needed?

3. *How will you substantiate the purpose for change?* Develop a substantial list of reasons why change is needed.

4. *How actively will you be involved in the change(s)?* List some ways to obtain commitments from other people to help address the components of change.

5. *How will you know that quality change has taken place?* Evaluation techniques must help you convince others that progress (or proper change) has taken place.

6. *Does your self-concept include an image of yourself as a change agent?* Are you committed to the role? How do you strengthen or maintain your role as change agent?

Activity: 10.8   Making Change Happen

In your group, develop an outline of steps that you must take to make the change from reactive guidance services to a proactive school counseling program. Use a flipchart or the chalkboard to record your results. Consider where leadership and supervision fit in.

Summary

In this chapter, we have covered the basics of leadership and supervision as they apply to comprehensive developmental school counseling program development. We have stressed that there are different kinds of leadership. As we promote cooperation and collaboration, and balance task and maintenance issues, we also need to assert leadership and promote student advocacy.

References

American School Counselor Association. (1990). *Role statement: The school counselor.* Alexandria, VA: Author.

American School Counselor Association. (1990). *School counselor competencies.* Alexandria, VA: Author.

Association for Counselor Education and Supervision. (1989, Spring). *ACES adopts standards for counseling supervisors* (pp. 8–11). Author.

Bernard, J., & Goodyear, R. (1998). *Fundamentals of clinical supervision* (2nd ed.). Boston: Allyn & Bacon.

Bucciantini, C. (1999). *Conceptual framework for clinical supervision in the Auburn school department.* Auburn, ME. Unpublished paper.

Dye, H. A., & Borders, L. D. (1990). Counseling supervisor: Standards for preparation and practice. *Journal of Counseling and Development, 69,* 27–29.

Fall, M. J. (1998, Spring). Clinical supervisor: The counselor's mechanic and technician. *Maine School Counselor Association Newsletter.*

Hersey, P., & Blanchard, K. H. (1992). *Leadership effectiveness and adaptability description (LEAD).* Escondido, CA: Leadership Studies.

Holloway, E. L., & Johnston, R. (1985). Group supervision: Widely practiced but poorly understood. *Counselor Education and Supervision, 24,* 332–340.

VanZandt, C. E. (1984, September). Counselor supervision: Putting the cart before the horse. *ACES Access, 44*(1), 14–15.

Reflections on Chapter 10

1. How is your job description similar to that of the director at Clover High School? How is it different?

2. With which leadership style are you most comfortable? Why?

3. Which of the supervision traits that your group identified do you believe you already have? Which will you need to work on?

4. What other terms might you use instead of *change agent*?

5. What questions do you have for yourself, your group members, or the facilitator of your group?

6. Notes:

Chapter 11

Ensuring Professional Development

Graduating from an approved Counselor Education Program that offers state certification in elementary and/or secondary school counseling is a beginning, a "commencement," into the counseling profession. Usually, this credential enables you to practice counseling in a public school. All professions recognize the importance of continuing education and other applications of professional development as an essential factor in maintaining the integrity of the profession. Counseling is like building a house; professional development is like decorating it, upgrading equipment, and remodeling.

The counseling profession has many ways to keep counselors current and competent to work with today's changing school populations. Professional development is both a group and an individual responsibility. The personnel involved in the comprehensive school counseling program will need to identify the knowledge and skill areas that everyone needs to address the systemic needs of the program. However, the professional development efforts must be balanced with individual plans that allow counselors to pursue areas of "personal mastery" (Senge, 1990).

In this chapter, we will help you explore several avenues for "sharpening the saw," as Covey (1989) described this process in his *7 Habits of Highly Effective People* (see Chapter 1). All states have, or are working on, requirements for mandatory professional development plans for educators. Truly professional educators do not bemoan such requirements; they embrace the concept as an integral part of their professional identity. The challenge for dedicated professionals is to try to limit the possibilities for professional development to a plausible list of high-priority actions. Figure 11.1 lists some of the typical categories and related skills that need to be considered in a professional development plan.

A MATTER OF COMPETENCE

The Ethical Standards for School Counselors (ASCA, 1998; see Appendix E) provides a powerful framework for understanding and addressing the individual obligations that are connected to professional development. Two sections in particular (section E, "Responsibilities to Self," and section F, "Responsibilities to the Profession") offer an excellent point of reference for the activities in this chapter.

126

Read each of the following statements, and circle the number that best describes (1) how important this competency is to the implementation of a comprehensive school counseling program and (2) how high your need is to improve this competency.

Importance	My Need
4 = Very Important	4 = Very High Need
3 = Important	3 = High Need
2 = Slightly Important	2 = Moderate Need
1 = Not Important	1 = Low Need

After you have rated each of the statements according to its importance for implementing a comprehensive guidance program and your need to improve this competency, review the statements that you rated for both very important and very high need and select the five that represent your most important inservice training needs. List them in the "Most Important Professional Development Needs" section at the end of the survey.

Thank you for taking the time to complete the form thoroughly.

Counseling and Consultation

1. Knowledge of general counseling and career development theories and techniques.

Importance	My Need
1 2 3 4	1 2 3 4

2. Knowledge of decision-making models.

Importance	My Need
1 2 3 4	1 2 3 4

3. Skills in building a productive relationship between counselor and client.

Importance	My Need
1 2 3 4	1 2 3 4

4. Skills in conducting group activities.

Importance	My Need
1 2 3 4	1 2 3 4

5. Skills in assisting students to deal with bias and stereotyping related to career decisions.

Importance	My Need
1 2 3 4	1 2 3 4

6. Ability to help students identify and pursue postsecondary educational, training, and employment opportunities.

Importance	My Need
1 2 3 4	1 2 3 4

7. Ability to assist students in selecting courses.

Importance	My Need
1 2 3 4	1 2 3 4

Figure 11.1 Self-assessment of counselor inservice training needs

8. Ability to assist students in the development of interpersonal skills.

	Importance	My Need
	1 2 3 4	1 2 3 4

9. Ability to assist students in matching developed academic skills with identified employment requirements.

	Importance	My Need
	1 2 3 4	1 2 3 4

10. Ability to assist students to interpret labor market information.

	Importance	My Need
	1 2 3 4	1 2 3 4

11. Ability to provide students with skills to manage their lives.

	Importance	My Need
	1 2 3 4	1 2 3 4

Information

12. Knowledge of the changing role of women and men and the linkage of work, family, and leisure.

	Importance	My Need
	1 2 3 4	1 2 3 4

13. Knowledge of strategies to store, retrieve, and disseminate career and occupational information.

	Importance	My Need
	1 2 3 4	1 2 3 4

14. Knowledge of educational trends and state and federal legislation.

	Importance	My Need
	1 2 3 4	1 2 3 4

15. Knowledge of state and local referral services/agencies.

	Importance	My Need
	1 2 3 4	1 2 3 4

Individual and Group Assessment

16. Knowledge and application of assessment techniques and measures of aptitudes, achievement, interest, values, and personality.

	Importance	My Need
	1 2 3 4	1 2 3 4

17. Ability to identify assessment resources appropriate for special populations.

	Importance	My Need
	1 2 3 4	1 2 3 4

Figure 11.1 Continued

18. Ability to identify assessment resources and techniques in terms of their validity, reliability, and relationships to race, sex, age, and ethnicity.

<pre>
        Importance   My Need
        1   2   3   4   1   2   3   4
</pre>

19. Ability to interpret and personalize assessment data.

<pre>
        Importance   My Need
        1   2   3   4   1   2   3   4
</pre>

Management and Administration

20. Knowledge of program designs that can be used in the organization of guidance programs.

<pre>
        Importance   My Need
        1   2   3   4   1   2   3   4
</pre>

21. Knowledge of needs assessment techniques and practices.

<pre>
        Importance   My Need
        1   2   3   4   1   2   3   4
</pre>

22. Ability to assess the effectiveness of current programs and practices.

<pre>
        Importance   My Need
        1   2   3   4   1   2   3   4
</pre>

23. Knowledge of leadership styles.

<pre>
        Importance   My Need
        1   2   3   4   1   2   3   4
</pre>

24. Ability to identify/develop and use record-keeping methods.

<pre>
        Importance   My Need
        1   2   3   4   1   2   3   4
</pre>

25. Ability to prepare proposals, budgets, and time lines.

<pre>
        Importance   My Need
        1 2 3 4 1   2   3   4   1   2   3   4
</pre>

26. Ability to evaluate program and student outcomes.

<pre>
        Importance   My Need
        1   2   3   4   1   2   3   4
</pre>

27. Ability to convey program goals and achievements to key personnel in positions of authority: legislators, executives, and others.

<pre>
        Importance   My Need
        1   2   3   4   1   2   3   4
</pre>

28. Ability to provide data on the cost-effectiveness of counseling programs.

<pre>
        Importance   My Need
        1   2   3   4   1   2   3   4
</pre>

Figure 11.1   Continued

Implementation

29. Ability to implement a public relations initiative for the guidance program.

           Importance   My Need

           1 2 3 4   1 2 3 4

30. Ability to manage a career resource center.

           Importance   My Need

           1 2 3 4   1 2 3 4

31. Ability to establish linkages with community-based organizations that provide placement services.

           Importance   My Need

           1 2 3 4   1 2 3 4

32. Knowledge of local and state employers as referral sources for employment opportunities.

           Importance   My Need

           1 2 3 4   1 2 3 4

Special Populations

33. Responsive to the unique issues and needs of minorities and other cultures.

           Importance   My Need

           1 2 3 4   1 2 3 4

34. Responsive to and knowledge of various handicapping conditions and necessary assistance and requirements.

           Importance   My Need

           1 2 3 4   1 2 3 4

35. Ability to identify community resources and establish linkages to assist students with special needs.

           Importance   My Need

           1 2 3 4   1 2 3 4

My Most Important Professional Development Needs:

1) # _____-_____

2) # _____-_____

3) # _____-_____

4) # _____-_____

5) # _____-_____

                                   Name_____

Figure 11.1 Continued

Source: *Self-Assessment of Counselor Inservice Training Needs,* 1990, by Belinda McCharen, State Guidance Coordinator, Oklahoma Department of Vocational and Technical Education, 1500 W. Seventh Avenue, Stillwater, OK 74074. Revised and reprinted with permission.

SECTION E. RESPONSIBILITIES TO SELF

E.1. Professional Competence

a. *The professional school counselor functions within the boundaries of individual professional competence and accepts responsibility for the consequences of his or her actions.*

Counselors need a variety of skills and competencies to implement a comprehensive school counseling program. A self-assessment will help you identify your current inservice training needs and develop an individual plan to improve your comprehensive school counseling program.

The form in Figure 11.1 is an adaptation of a survey originally developed by career and vocational counselors working with Belinda McCharen, State Guidance Coordinator, Oklahoma Department of Vocational and Technical Education in Stillwater, Oklahoma. The survey was administered to practicing school counselors in the state of Oklahoma. The results were summarized, a profile was developed, and a mid-winter conference was planned to address the needs defined in this self-assessment.

Activity 11.1   Self-Assessment of Counselor Inservice Training Needs

Individually, complete the self-assessment in Figure 11.1. Then, in your group, after each person has identified his or her "Most Important Professional Development Needs," try to come to a consensus on the group's top three priority needs. What are the implications for future responsibilities related to professional development?

> Continuing professional involvement makes it possible for counselors to grow and improve as practitioners. . . . Excellent resources and opportunities are provided for inservice training, individualized enrichment through reading and collegial support groups, requirements for continued credentialing, advanced degree programs, and other special services. It is professionalism, however, which motivates a counselor to take advantage of and to use the opportunities that are provided in these areas. Mandated, generic, staff development programs are not sufficient for counselors with professionalism; a personal plan of action is valued and pursued. (VanZandt, 1990, p. 244)

b. *The professional school counselor monitors personal functioning and effectiveness and does not participate in any activity which may lead to inadequate professional services or harm to a client.*

Activity 11.2   Button Pushing

Identify the kinds of situations or behaviors that "push your buttons," that is, the times when your personal issues make it less likely that students will receive the best services. For example, a counselor whose own child has had difficulty with drugs may find it difficult to refrain from lecturing or moralizing.

1. Create a scenario that describes a personal issue—yours or someone else's.

2. Brainstorm with your group some ways to address the challenges this scenario presents.

c. *The professional school counselor strives through personal initiative to maintain professional competence and keep abreast of professional information. Professional and personal growth are ongoing throughout the counselor's career.*

Activity 11.3 Innovations and Trends

In a small group, create a list of five to ten topics that reflect current issues or trends in the field of school counseling today. Base your choices on professional journal articles and newsletters, government reports, state mandates, the popular press, and so on. As a group, try to reach a consensus about which three topics are the most important.

1.

2.

3.

4.

5.

6.

7.

8.

9.

10.

E.2. Multicultural Skills

The professional school counselor understands the diverse cultural backgrounds of the counselees with whom he/she works. This includes, but is not limited to, learning how the school counselor's own cultural/ethnic/racial identity impacts her or his values and beliefs about the counseling process.

Activity 11.4   Facing One's Own Diversity

1. Take the pretest on multicultural counseling competencies in Chapter 6, Figure 6.3. Which area of competency provides the greatest challenge for you?

How will you begin to address this challenge?

SECTION F. RESPONSIBILITIES TO THE PROFESSION

F.1. Professionalism

a.   *The professional school counselor accepts the policies and processes for handling ethical violations as a result of maintaining membership in the American School Counseling Association.*

Because the message is so obvious, we are not even going to provide an activity here. You need to apply the ASCA Ethical Standards as they are published in Appendix E, but be aware that they may be updated at any time.

b.   *The professional school counselor conducts herself/himself in such a manner as to advance ethical practice and the profession.*

Activity 11.5   Dual Relationships

In small groups, generate a list of possible dual relationships that may cause challenges to the profession's image (for example, a counselor drinking alcohol at a party at which the host's children, who are part of the counselor's caseload, are present).

c.   *The professional school counselor conducts appropriate research and reports findings in a manner consistent with acceptable educational and psychological research practices. When using client data for research or for statistical or program planning purposes, the counselor ensures protection of the individual counselee's identity.*

Activity 11.6   Setting Up a Follow-Up Study

In small groups, outline on newsprint the process that you will use to conduct a follow-up study of recent graduates. What parameters will you set to acquire information that will help you determine the changes that need to be made in your current program? Describe how you will protect individual students.

d.   *The professional school counselor adheres to ethical standards of the profession, other official policy statements pertaining to counseling, and relevant statutes established by federal, state and local governments.*

Activity 11.7   Examining Other Policy Statements

Several organizations have ethical standards and policy statements that are relevant to school counseling. The American Psychological Association, for example, has several statements that overlap or may even appear to be contradictory to the ASCA standards. Discuss any policies from other organizations that seem to place the school counselor in conflict with local or national counseling standards. One example with which to begin might be student confidentiality versus the good of the organization.

e.   *The professional school counselor clearly distinguishes between statements and actions as a private individual and those made as a representative of the school counseling profession.*

Activity 11.8 Be Yourself

Develop a scenario in which you, the counselor, must state an opinion or act as a private individual in a situation that seems oppositional to your behavior as a school counselor. For example, suppose you are on the school drug and alcohol abuse committee and you are seen leaving a local bar by a parent who is also on that committee. What would you say? How would you act?

f.   *The professional school counselor does not use his or her professional position to recruit or gain clients, consultees for her or his private practice, seek and receive unjustified personal gain, unfair advantage, sexual favors, or unearned goods or services.*

Activity 11.9 Beyond Mediocrity

To move beyond mediocrity, a "must-read" text is Stephen Covey's book, *The 7 Habits of Highly Effective People* (see Chapter 1 for a discussion of this text). Write a paper in which you relate the concepts in this book to the effectiveness of professional school counselors, and in which you compare and contrast Covey's message with messages you read in other texts and related resources. The paper is to be entitled *My Personal Vision of Professional Effectiveness*. In your paper, use Covey's concepts and your own vision of personal effectiveness to:

1. Create a personal mission statement.
2. Identify the ten most significant competencies you must possess to be not only an effective school counselor but an *excellent* one.
3. Describe the kind of image you want to project as a school counselor and the kind of image you want your program to have. (Begin with the end in mind!)
4. Describe how you personally plan to stay committed to professional excellence.
5. Identify the most important idea or concept you have learned from Covey. Also identify what have you learned about yourself as you have reflected on the seven habits.

This exercise is extremely important. Our students, who are required to do this exercise, always remark how much the exercise helps them to analyze and synthesize the *most important* aspects of their development as school counselors. The following quote is taken from one student's list of competencies; it illustrates the connection between acceptance and awareness of one's personal characteristics:

Self-awareness is fundamental to a counselor's ability to function with integrity and effectiveness, regardless of the setting. An understanding of one's strengths and weaknesses, biases, interests, and inclinations is necessary to maintain balance and perspective when it comes to interpersonal relationships with all of our constituencies: students, parents, teachers, administrators, fellow counselors, and community members. Who we are as a counselor is not just a reflection of theoretical perspective and personality; it is the result of a conscious decision concerning what kind of person we want and choose to be—on and off the job.

As Michael Cavanagh so aptly puts it in *The Counseling Experience*, "Self-knowledge means the counselors know themselves well enough that they almost always know exactly what they are doing, why they are doing it, which problems are theirs, and which belong to the person in counseling." To be effective in a school setting we must be honest with our expectations of ourselves in terms of commitment, energy, creativity, and objectivity before we can realistically assess the needs of our setting and formulate a plan in which we are to be agents of change. (Susan K. Tree, 1988)

F.2. Contribution to the Profession

a. *The professional school counselor actively participates in local, state and national associations which foster the development and improvement of school counseling.*

Activity 11.10   Join Your Counseling Associations

Determine which local, statewide, and national associations are addressing the goals of your own school district and join as a dues-paying member. Many professional associations have reduced membership fees for students; this is a good way to try out an association to determine whether it fits your needs. Depending upon your own interests and work setting, you might consider the school counseling association, multicultural counseling association, career development association, or the association of counselor educators and supervisors—to name only a few. Talk with individuals who already belong to one or more of these organizations to determine where you might fit best. Ask them to invite you to a conference or a board meeting. We are suggesting that you at least join a statewide organization if you find the costs for joining a national organization to be beyond your means.

b. *The professional school counselor contributes to the development of the profession through the sharing of skills, ideas and expertise with colleagues.*

Activity 11.11   Share the Wealth

Please refer to Chapter 7, activities 7.3 and 7.4. Set up a brief workshop for your colleagues so that you can share information with them that you obtained at a recent workshop or conference you attended. Provide an activity at your workshop that you experienced at the conference and really liked. Be sure to share handouts, as well.

You have now read two sections (sections E and F) of the ASCA Ethical Standards for School Counselors during your exploration of professional development initiatives. Please refer to Appendix E to more thoroughly examine your ethical obligations and professional development responsibilities. You may choose to write activities for some of the other ethical standards.

PROFESSIONAL DEVELOPMENT FOR YOUR SCHOOL COUNSELING TEAM

Although it is important for you to develop your own individual competencies, it is also important that your school counseling team pay attention to the big picture—that is, how you are collectively delivering your program and nurturing yourselves as a professional team. In the following activities, explore how you will pool your resources for nurturing your development as a learning community, which in turn will serve as a model for the rest of the school.

Activity 11.12   Identifying Competencies

As a team, identify no more than ten professional development competencies that you, as a team, do not have but which need attention in a comprehensive guidance and counseling program.

1. _____
2. _____

3. _____
4. _____
5. _____
6. _____
7. _____
8. _____
9. _____
10. _____

What are some questions that your team needs to ask itself about these competencies? For example, does every member of your team need all of these competencies?

1. _____
2. _____
3. _____

In the following text, we will identify some sources of providing staff development and training to help counselors reach their maximum potential. Before scanning our list, please identify some methods that you believe will contribute to your own and your team's competencies. P.S. We found ten. Good luck.

1. _____
2. _____
3. _____
4. _____
5. _____
6. _____
7. _____
8. _____
9. _____
10. _____

Here are the ten staff development sources and initiatives that we determined could be used to enhance present counselor competencies. How does your list compare with ours?

1. Individual group members. Often, an individual within a team has an area of expertise that he or she can teach to others.
2. Community agencies. Resources such as mental health centers sometimes present staff development training workshops led by experts in the field.
3. Professional trainers. Increasingly, professionals are packaging their expertise and offering staff development training workshops independent of an agency or organization.
4. Colleges and universities. Usually considered a traditional provider of courses and programs, most colleges also offer conferences and workshops intended to enhance the counselor's expertise. When an accredited institution changes its degree program, graduates of the program should return, if possible, and attend any new, required courses in order to remain current.
5. Business and industry. Participating in pertinent workshops and seminars offered by business and industry provides not only training but also an opportunity for counselor interaction with the community.
6. Professional organizations. Membership in professional organizations at the national level—the American Counseling Association (ACA) and the American

School Counselor Association (ASCA)—and their state and local branches will make available many professional development opportunities.

7. Governmental agencies. Local, state, and federal government agencies, such as your State Department of Education, often sponsor training and development for specific programs.

8. Outside consultants. Sometimes a school district or a group within a school district identifies a need for some very specific training or group problem solving by a skilled trainer in that field.

9. Publishing articles. You will find that your own skills are enhanced as you attempt to explain and synthesize your ideas in meaningful journal articles.

10. Reading books and journal articles.

Activity 11.13   Staff Development Examples

In your groups, list some specific examples of the ten sources of staff development training that we just provided. List at least one example for each source.

1. *Example: Counselor presents workshop on a learning styles inventory with which she has* _____
   expertise. _____

2. _____

3. _____

4. *Example: Summer courses at the university in suicide prevention.* _____

5. _____

6. _____

7. _____

8. _____

9. _____

10. _____

BEYOND MEDIOCRITY

Many school counseling programs view minimum standards as maximum standards. You would not want counselors serving your own children to possess such an attitude toward their jobs, would you? You need to think about how your school counseling program demonstrates that mediocrity is not the norm for your staff. One of our course requirements, and certainly something for practitioners to consider doing, is to write a brief paper about excellence in counseling. Professional development is the avenue by which we can avoid mediocrity and continue to build personal mastery and program excellence.

Summary

In this chapter, we have highlighted the importance of educators staying current with, or even a bit ahead of, the complex challenges that confront us in today's society. Because we are first and foremost student advocates, it behooves us not only to keep ourselves ahead of the curve, but to bring others along with us.

References

American School Counselor Association. (1998). *Ethical standards for school counselors.* Alexandria, VA: Author.

Covey, S. R. (1989). *The 7 habits of highly effective people.* New York, NY: Simon and Schuster, Inc.

Senge, P. (1990). *The fifth discipline: The art & practice of the learning organization.* New York: Currency Doubleday.

VanZandt, C. E. (1990). Professionalism: A matter of personal initiative. *Journal of Counseling and Development, 68,* 243–245.

Reflections on Chapter 11

1. Have you already identified specific topics or areas of learning where your counselor training program did not provide the level of expertise to allow you to perform competently and ethically? What are those areas or topics?

2. How do you feel about the progress of your group?

3. How do you feel about your role in your group?

4. Could you identify areas of need for some of your group members? How would you approach the task of making them aware of their needs?

5. What questions do you have for yourself, your group, or your group facilitator?

6. Notes:

✞ Chapter 12
Conducting Program Evaluation

Too often the word *evaluation* brings about task-avoidance tendencies in education. Although most people understand and appreciate the need to conduct evaluations and use applied research in their work, many people feel inadequately prepared to live up to the challenges of reliability and validity. In this handbook, however, you have already laid the foundation for valid evaluation procedures. You have completed some important applied research as you conducted the needs assessment in your school/district. The results yielded useful information for planning and developing your comprehensive guidance program. Perhaps the needs assessment also gave you information about what is already being taught, and being learned, in your program, as well as information about what people perceive as needs that are not being addressed. Such information can now provide the focus for assessing the effectiveness of your program.

As you may recall from the discussion in Chapter 1 about accountability, it is important to think about reporting "meaningful information about program needs and accomplishments. . . ." Reporting program accomplishments, or the lack thereof, is the very essence of program evaluation. Without a well-thought-out and thorough evaluation plan, program accountability is rendered as a meaningless concept.

Evaluation needs to be approached from two different perspectives: formative and summative. *Formative* evaluations provide information during the development and implementation phases of the program. Such information *informs* us about our needs and program highlights. *Summative* evaluations are more descriptive; they tell us what the program has accomplished and are usually aligned with the program goals.

As you develop and implement your program, ongoing formative evaluation is extremely important. Instruments need to be developed and applied that measure the extent to which the identified outcomes are being met. It is not enough to say that the topics are being taught; we need to provide reasonable proof that the competencies are being learned by the students in a useful manner. Once the outcomes are measured or evaluated, you not only report on the level of attainment of these objectives, but you also set new or refined outcomes based upon this data.

FRAMEWORK FOR PROGRAM EVALUATION

In Chapter 4, several program models were described, and then you were challenged to create your own model (borrowing liberally from those that were presented, we assume). We are going to highlight the Missouri model in this discussion about evaluation, since Maine and New Hampshire have adopted this model. This brief discussion of how evaluation is integrated in all four components of the Missouri model is offered to illustrate the range of evaluation strategies that are possible, and to help you consider some plausible options for creating your own evaluation plan. If you are using a model that differs from the Missouri model, you will just need to adapt the ideas to fit your own framework for program delivery. Once again, the four components of the Missouri model are: guidance curriculum, individual planning, responsive services, and program management.

THE GUIDANCE CURRICULUM

Evaluation of the guidance curriculum requires both formative and summative information. Refer to the scope and sequence grid that you set up in Chapter 6. In developing that chart, you should have fully developed your learning outcomes, identified who will teach these learning outcomes, and determined where and when they are to be integrated in the curriculum.

Formative information you have collected throughout the year might include feedback from teachers and students about the quality of the content and delivery of the curriculum. Summative information at the end of the year might include a listing of the number of classroom guidance lessons presented and the number of students participating, evidence of outcome attainment, and summaries of student ratings.

Activity 12.1   Student Competency Evaluation

In order to develop student competency evaluations, refer to your needs assessment results from Chapter 5. Ask yourself the following questions.

1. What did the teachers, students, and community identify as priority needs?

2. How thoroughly were competencies outlined for each area of need?

3. Were the competencies covered either in the guidance curriculum or in another organized curriculum?

4. How will you know that the students have learned these competencies?

One way to determine whether your students have learned the competencies is to have them take five minutes or so at the end of a class to respond anonymously and in writing to an evaluation (Figure 12.1).

INDIVIDUAL PLANNING

As with guidance curriculum evaluation, you will need both quantitative and qualitative information. For quantitative measures, a simple grid with student names, coded if necessary, will probably be sufficient. Illustrate how your program includes all students. For example, a checklist could demonstrate that each student has been met, how often, and for what reason.

Qualitative evaluations of individual planning are somewhat more complex. However, one excellent method of meeting the qualitative criteria is through the use of student portfolios. Portfolios can show how you have worked with all students—individually and in groups or classes—and how the students have developed goals, have been involved in activities, and have met benchmarks in achieving their goals. One excellent resource for portfolio building is the *Get a Life Portfolio* (VanZandt, Perry, & Brawley, 1993) developed by the American School Counselor Association (ASCA) with support from the National Occupational Information Coordinating Committee (NOICC).

Name of Lesson: _____   Date: _____

1.   What did you learn from this activity?

2.   What would you have the instructor do differently?

3.   How will you use this new information?

Figure 12.1 Student activity evaluation

A distinct advantage of using the student portfolio as a qualitative evaluation is that it puts the responsibility for success directly in the students' hands.

RESPONSIVE SERVICES

One of the major challenges of evaluating responsive services is in differentiating preventative services from those interventions that are seen as more reactive. For example, counselors may want to list the number of small groups they have created for addressing typical developmental concerns and classify those as preventative strategies. However, they may also want to create a separate list of groups they lead for students who are experiencing crises or problems that are significantly interfering with their performance in school. Counselors need to portray an accurate picture of the severity of issues with which some students are dealing if they are to get the support they need to meet the needs of such students. Most people, including many teachers within the schools, are not aware of the severity of mental health issues students bring to school. It is possible to shed some light on such needs without disclosing confidential information, but counselors must be sensitive to what will be "meaningful information" for such people. Time and task analyses for both preventative and crisis responsive services can provide information about personnel needs, as well as the balancing of the counselors' time.

Evaluation of responsive services can be both quantitative and qualitative. The model that we have used for responsive services is primarily preventative. By addressing responsive services through both guidance curriculum and individual planning, we are trying to ensure that we meet the needs of most students before these needs emerge as crises. We need to at least provide data about the number of preventive responsive services we are providing for students.

School counselors also work with students who need assistance beyond the regular classroom or counseling office. An up-to-date repertoire of referral sources is an important second line of defense for addressing a variety of student needs. We suggest that counselors document the use of referral sources and that they also clarify the nature and severity of the issues that have been referred to outside resources.

As a final example of evaluating responsive services, school counseling programs also need to describe how their crisis management plan has operated during the year. Although it may only be used once or twice a year, an assessment of the efficiency and effectiveness of the plan can lead to improved services in coming years.

SYSTEM SUPPORT/PROGRAM MANAGEMENT

There are several evaluation strategies that can enhance the effectiveness of the entire operation of the program. The most important factor, however, in evaluating this component of the program is the program leader's ability to be open (and vulnerable) and receptive to feedback.

Following are two activities that address important issues in the evaluation of the system support/program management component. In three separate groups, complete one of the following activities, and then try out your evaluation on the other two groups. You will need to explain the evaluation procedure before involving the group members in the activity.

Activity 12.2 Evaluating Financial Resources

In Chapter 8, you were asked to develop a guidance program budget. Now, look back at that budget and design an evaluation that will enable you to report to your school board that the funds are being appropriately spent. This evaluation can be a simple five- or six-question form. An important aspect of this evaluation is that, with this information, you will be able to justify your budget and, perhaps, an increase for the following year as well.

Activity 12.3 School Counselor Performance Appraisal

Too often the performance of school counselors is measured using the same checklist/instrument as that used for teachers. We contend that although the teaching role is embedded in much of what the counselor does, the separate responsibilities of the counselor require a different evaluation instrument. Rather than ask you to design

---

INSTRUCTIONS:

1. The evaluator is to rate the school counselor on a four-point scale as indicated below.
2. The evaluator is encouraged to add pertinent comments at the end of each major function.
3. The school counselor is provided an opportunity to react to the evaluator's ratings and comments.
4. The evaluator and the school counselor must discuss the results of the appraisal and any recommended action pertinent to it.
5. Both the evaluator and the school counselor sign the instrument in the assigned spaces.

School Counselor's Name _____

School _____

0	Not applicable
1	Performs unsatisfactorily
2	Needs improvement in performance
3	Meets performance expectations
4	Exceeds performance expectations

A. Major Function: Manages the School Guidance and Counseling Program

　　1. Assists in developing a comprehensive developmental school guidance and counseling plan that is based on student needs.　　0　1　2　3　4

　　2. Develops activities, resources, and time lines to implement the goals and objectives of the comprehensive school guidance and counseling program plan.　　0　1　2　3　4

　　3. Involves school personnel in the decision-making process related to implementing a comprehensive guidance program through an advisory committee and other relevant techniques.　　0　1　2　3　4

　　4. Conducts regular public awareness initiatives to highlight guidance and counseling program activities, services, and accomplishments.　　0　1　2　3　4

Comments: _____

B. Major Function: Provides Individual Counseling

　　1. Provides individual counseling for students to meet their remedial, preventive, and developmental needs.　　0　1　2　3　4

　　2. Demonstrates positive human relationships by showing respect for the worth and dignity of all students from all cultural backgrounds.　　0　1　2　3　4

Figure 12.2　School counselor performance appraisal instrument

3. Shares appropriate information with school personnel, parents, and community agencies about the needs and concerns of students.　　0　1　2　3　4
4. Networks with community agencies as needed.　　0　1　2　3　4

Comments: _____

C. Major Function: Provides Group Counseling and Guidance

1. Provides group counseling for students to meet their remedial, preventive, and developmental needs.　　0　1　2　3　4
2. Assesses the progress of students in group counseling and evaluates the overall effectiveness of the group counseling interventions.　　0　1　2　3　4

Comments: _____

D. Major Function: Provides Classroom Guidance

1. Collaborates with classroom teachers to provide a classroom developmental guidance curriculum in the area of personal/ social, educational, and career development.　　0　1　2　3　4
2. Provides classroom guidance lessons that are developmentally appropriate.　　0　1　2　3　4
3. Uses teaching and classroom management strategies that are conducive to learning.　　0　1　2　3　4
4. Assesses the effectiveness of the classroom guidance curriculum.　　0　1　2　3　4

Comments _____

E. Major Function: Assists in Providing for Students' Career Development

1. Provides an up-to-date career and vocational information system or resource center appropriate to the age of the students.　　0　1　2　3　4
2. Assists students in achieving successful educational and vocational placement based on aptitude, achievement, and interest.　　0　1　2　3　4
3. Provides parents with information and programs that help meet the career needs of students.　　0　1　2　3　4
4. Assists in the coordination of career portfolios that help students integrate their career experiences.　　0　1　2　3　4
5. Assists in coordinating efforts of business, industry, and civic organizations to provide career opportunities for students.　　0　1　2　3　4

Comments: _____

F. Major Function: Provides Consultation Services

1. Describes the nature of consultation services to faculty and parents.　　0　1　2　3　4
2. Helps teachers and parents meet the specialized needs of students through mutual problem-solving techniques.　　0　1　2　3　4

Comments: _____

Figure 12.2 Continued

G. Major Function: Assists in Gathering and Utilizing Student Assessment Information

    1. Assists in implementing assessment programs and student
        evaluation procedures.   0 1 2 3 4
    2. Assists school personnel, parents, and students in evaluating,
        interpreting, and utilizing test scores and other student data
        in order to meet student needs.   0 1 2 3 4

Comments: _____

H. Major Function: Keeps Own Professional Competence Current

    1. Updates professional growth and development plan.   0 1 2 3 4
    2. Engages in professional development opportunities.   0 1 2 3 4
    3. Operates according to the ethical code of the counseling
        profession.   0 1 2 3 4

Comments: _____

Evaluator's Summary Comments: _____

_____

_____

School Counselor's Reactions to Evaluation: _____

_____

_____

_____   _____
Evaluator's Signature/Title   Date

_____   _____
Counselor's Signature   Date

Signature indicates that the written evaluation has been seen and discussed.

Figure 12.2 Continued

Source: Adapted from an instrument developed by Kathryn VanZandt, Director of Guidance Programs, Windham High School, Windham, Maine.

one, we are including a sample high school counselor performance appraisal instrument for you to modify if you wish (Figure 12.2).

Activity 12.4 Evaluating Your Program

Using texts (Carr, Brook, Hayslip, Williams, & Zwolinski, 1997; Gysbers & Henderson, 2000; Myrick, 1996) as references, design a survey instrument that will yield an evaluation of your entire school counseling program. Your survey will likely be organized around the four program components: guidance curriculum, individual planning, responsive services, and system support. We suggest that you refer back to your time and task analysis and your needs assessment documents (Chapter 5) to form the baseline for your survey. In addition to using your texts, you may want to refer to *Evaluating Guidance Programs: A Practitioner's Guide* (Johnson & Whitfield, 1991); *Leading and Managing Your School Guidance Program Staff: A Manual for Building and District Administrators* (Henderson & Gysbers, 1998); and an excellent article entitled "Improving School Guidance Programs: A Framework for Program, Personnel, and Results Evaluation" (Gysbers, Hughey, Starr, & Lapan, 1992).

Finally, those who are being evaluated need to know what they are being evaluated for and how the results will be used. Furthermore, evaluating the program elements as they are applied will enable you to make some fine-tuning changes during the school year.

Summary

In this chapter we have given you some references and examples of program and personnel evaluation. We hope that you will develop evaluations from these models that will meet your specific program needs.

References

Carr, J. V., Brook, C. A., Hayslip, J. B., Williams, F., & Zwolinski, M. (1997). *A manual for comprehensive career guidance and counseling program.* Derry, NH: New Hampshire Comprehensive Guidance and Counseling Program, Inc.

Gysbers, N. C., & Henderson, P. (1997). *Comprehensive guidance programs that work—II.* Greensboro, NC: ERIC Counseling and Student Services Clearinghouse.

Gysbers, N. C., & Henderson, P. (2000). *Developing and managing your school guidance program* (3rd ed.). Alexandria, VA: American Association for Counseling and Development.

Gysbers, N. C., Hughey, K. F., Starr, M., & Lapan, R. T. (1992). Improving school guidance programs: A framework for program, personnel, and results evaluation. *Journal of Counseling and Development, 70,* 565–570.

Henderson, P., & Gysbers, N. C. (1998). *Leading and managing your school guidance program staff: A manual for building and district administrators.* Alexandria, VA: American Association for Counseling and Development.

Johnson, S. K., & Whitfield, E. A. (1991). *Evaluating guidance programs: A practitioner's guide.* Iowa City, IA: ACT and the National Consortium of State Career Guidance Supervisors.

Myrick, R. D. (1996). *Developmental guidance and counseling.* Minneapolis, MN: Educational Media Corp.

VanZandt, Z., Perry, N., & Brawley, K. (1993). *Get a life: Your personal planning portfolio.* Alexandria, VA: American School Counselor Association.

Reflections on Chapter 12

1. How satisfied are you with your group's evolving comprehensive development school guidance and counseling program?

2. How do you feel about individual group members' contributions?

3. What evaluation technique would you use to assess your group's process and products?

4. How do you feel about your role in your group?

5. What questions do you have for yourself, your group, or your group facilitator?

6. Notes:

✝ Chapter 13
Humanizing Technology

> In our minds, at least, technology is always on the verge of liberating us from
> personal discipline and responsibility. Only it never does and never will. The
> more high technology around us, the more the need for human touch.
>
> Naisbett (1982), Megatrends, p. 53

It goes without saying that we are in an age of technology—but we say it anyway.
Technology touches our lives in ways we could only imagine just a decade ago. While
technology introduces us to new opportunities and in many ways "liberates" us as we do
our work, it also presents us with many challenges as we consider its place in a comprehensive developmental school counseling program.

In this chapter, we want you to ponder some of the ways that technology can enhance your job, as well as empower youth in their development. On the other hand, we
also want you to examine some of the pitfalls and potential problem areas that may need
consideration. Finally, we will have you examine your professional development needs
in relation to technology so you can align some of your future educational goals with a
balanced high-tech/high-touch framework.

TECHNICAL COMPETENCIES

In recent years, counselors and counselor educators have examined some of the ethical
and pedagogical responsibilities related to the use of technology in the counseling field.
In 1999, the Technology Interest Network of the Association for Counselor Education and
Supervision (ACES) developed a list of competencies that were deemed as critical for
counselors to possess for successful integration of technology in our professional practice.
Focusing on preservice education, the interest network offered the recommendations
listed in Figure 13.1.

Although the purposes and parameters of this chapter do not allow us to thoroughly
focus on each of the competencies offered by the ACES recommendations, we will
nonetheless highlight certain areas as a means of exploring some of the complexities of
using technology in the school counselor's office.

At the completion of a counselor education program, all students should be:

1. able to use productivity software to develop web pages, group presentations, letters, reports, etc.
2. able to use such audiovisual equipment as video recorders, audio recorders, projection equipment, videoconferencing equipment, and playback units.
3. able to use computerized statistical packages.
4. able to use computerized testing, diagnostic, and career decision-making programs with clients.
5. able to use e-mail.
6. able to help clients search for various types of counseling-related information via the Internet, including information about careers, employment opportunities, educational and training opportunities, financial assistance/scholarships, treatment procedures, and social and personal information.
7. able to subscribe, participate in, and sign off counseling-related listservs.
8. able to access and use counseling and related CD-ROM databases.
9. knowledgeable of the legal and ethical codes that relate to counseling services via the Internet.
10. knowledgeable of the strengths and weaknesses of counseling services provided via the Internet.
11. able to use the Internet for finding and using continuing education opportunities in counseling.
12. able to evaluate the quality of Internet information.

Figure 13.1   Recommended technical competencies for counselor education students

PROGRAM CONNECTIONS

From word processing to web pages to data analysis to video cameras, technology has many applications in a comprehensive developmental school counseling program. Rather than spelling out all the possible applications, however, we want you to use your own resourcefulness and critical thinking to examine the various ways you could or should apply technology to make your program more effective and efficient. Besides, we are convinced that a greater synergy of thinking and learning can result from you pooling your knowledge and resources than if we were to just write a bunch of words on a page. The chapters in this book provide an excellent structure for exploring these possibilities in this next activity.

Activity 13.1   Connecting Technology

In your group, brainstorm specific examples that illustrate how technology could contribute to the following aspects of your comprehensive developmental school counseling program.

ACCOUNTABILITY

TEAMWORK

SYSTEMIC THINKING (seeing the big picture)

PROGRAM MODEL

NEEDS ASSESSMENT

CURRICULUM

DELEGATING RESPONSIBILITY

INSERVICE EDUCATION

ADVISORY COMMITTEE

BUDGET/GRANT WRITING

PUBLIC AWARENESS AND SUPPORT

PROFESSIONAL DEVELOPMENT

PROGRAM EVALUATION

PROGRAM DELIVERY

As your group reflects on the various ways that technology could be a part of your comprehensive developmental program, what are the management implications?

PERSONALIZING TECHNOLOGY

Keeping in mind that the human factor is still a critical element for success even in the use of technology, in the next few exercises we are going to focus on ways that school counselors can create a more personal approach to using technology.

Listservs

A listserv is created to link people with similar interests so that they can regularly share information, resources, and ideas through computer-assisted technology. Listservs provide a reasonably easy method for communicating via the Internet, and even those of us who are "technologically challenged" can follow a few simple instructions and become a part of a support system that meets our professional needs and/or personal styles.

Activity 13.2   Networking

This activity requires both individual and group initiative.

1. If you have not already done so, obtain authorization to use a computer system that has access to the Internet. Most schools, colleges, and universities have computer centers where you can access such a system. Authorization usually requires you to use your student or faculty identification number and a personal information number (PIN), which is assigned to you. You will then be given an e-mail address. The school will either set up an e-mail account or orient you to its system of accounting. Computer centers are almost always staffed with people who can lead you through the explanations and orientations that will make this task fairly easy.

2. Once everyone in your group is "authorized," share your e-mail addresses. Ask the person in your group who is most computer literate to help set up a listserv for your team. A listserv allows you to post a message that goes out to everyone on the list at the same time. (You also receive any messages that are posted by others.) While you are working to develop your comprehensive developmental school counseling program, use your group's listserv to make weekly "postings" about your progress, concerns, needs, insights, discoveries, and/or personal reflections related to your team's plan.

3. Join at least one national listserv related to the counseling profession. We suggest you start with the International Counseling Network by sending an e-mail message to: ICN@listserv.utk.edu. In the message, just write the words: Subscribe ICN. Once you have sent the message, it will not be long before you receive a reply that says you are now subscribed to the International Counseling Network. It is that simple. Remember that thereafter any message you send to the listserv will go to everyone who has signed on. If you wish to communicate with individuals who have posted messages on the listserv, but you do not care to have everyone "listen in" on your conversation, then you will need to send your message directly to the individual's e-mail address. Share the addresses of the listservs that you join with your group members.

4. Have a discussion in your group about one of the dialogues that has taken place on the listserv you have joined. Also, discuss how your participation on the listserv has helped to create a more personal link to the greater counseling community.

Websites

The Internet has an almost endless array of websites that are designed for a variety of purposes—the most noble of these being to provide information. The website is one area of technology where you must balance the benefits with caution regarding the pitfalls. Because we trust the collective experience and wisdom of the members of a group over the judgment of any individual, we want you to use the following activity to appreciate the pros and cons of using websites in your work.

Activity 13.3   Consumer Beware

In your group, generate a list of cautions that should be observed by counselors as they use the Internet. Keep in mind that some websites provide information resources; others sell products; and still others provide services such as web counseling. There are a host of other purposes that we do not even mention here.

   If more than one group is working on this activity, share your lists in the larger group. Reach agreement on the cautions that are necessary and significant.

Activity 13.4   Good Stuff

In Figure 13.2, we provide you a list of addresses for some of the websites related to the school counseling profession. Each person in your group should investigate at least two of the sites (decide which ones each member will investigate before you head out into cyberspace). As you explore your websites, reflect on the following questions:

- What do I like about this website?
- What is missing?
- For whom would this site be most useful?
- Should I recommend this website to others? Why or why not?

When you come back together as a group, share your reflections, insights, and especially the "good stuff" you have discovered.

A recent National Career Development Association (NCDA) publication, *The Internet: A Tool for Career Planning* (Harris-Bowlsby, Dikel, & Sampson, 1998), contains an annotated list of many websites.

Start each address with http://

- www.schoolcounselor.com

- www.counseling.org

- www.schoolcounselor.org

- www.bjpinchbeck.com (homework helper)

- npin.org (National Parent Information Network)

- www.webring.org (peer education)

- ssc.salkeiz.k12.or.us/counsel/ (School Counselor Program Home Page)

- www.humormatters.com/index.html (therapeutic humor)

- www.kiersey.com (Kiersey Temperament)

- http://stats.bls.gov/emphome.htm (Occupational Outlook Handbook)

- www.afsp.org (suicide prevention)

- www.petersons.com/ (colleges, etc.)

- www.careermosaic.com

- www.militarycareers.com

- curry.edschool.virginia.edu/curry/centers/multicultural/home.html

- idealist.com/cayp/index.shtml (child abuse)

- www.amhca.org (Mental Health Counselors)

- www.uncg.edu/edu/ericcass (ERIC Clearinghouse: Counseling and Student Services)

- www.futurescan.com (careers for teens)

- ncda.org (National Career Development Association)

Figure 13.2   List of websites for school counselors

Home Pages

Although many people now have their own web pages, creating websites is still a bit daunting for many of us who do not feel competent enough to create such a resource. The concept of a home page is essentially a means of humanizing the website. If a school counseling program creates its own home page in the school's website, the connection provided is more intimate than that created by just lumping the counseling program's information together with all the personnel and program information in the school's website. Likewise, within the counseling office, if the professional and clerical staff members each have individual home pages, students, parents, faculty, and members of the community will be able to see a more personal side of each individual before meeting that person face to face.

Activity 13.5   Home Is Where the Human Factor Is

1. In your group, brainstorm the kinds of things a school counselor might include in his or her home page.
2. As a homework assignment, identify what you would like to include in your home page (if you have not already created one; if you have one already, identify ways you will improve it). Decide whether you will create your own home page (which may require the development of some new knowledge and skill through training or self-study), pay to have one made for you, submit your ideas to your local webmaster, or wait until you are able to have a page created for you.

CHANGING TECHNOLOGY

Computer technology is outdated the minute it comes on the market. The technology industry regularly discovers new applications and ponders new theories and possibilities for how computers will be used in the future. As school counselors, we must know enough about the changing world of technology to help our students understand how they can prepare for change, make wise choices, ponder their futures, and develop competence for success in life. No one expects us to know everything about technology; if we did, we would be engineers instead of counselors. However, students need for us to understand the big picture of technology so we can help them make sense of their world; and we need to understand how we can use technology to be more effective and efficient as counselors. This challenge requires that we regularly assess our professional development needs in the area of technology.

Activity 13.6   Recognizing Our Needs

Review the list of recommended technical competencies in Figure 13.1. Identify the two areas that deserve the most attention in your professional development plans in the near future, both because of their importance and because of your need for improved knowledge and skill. List them here:

1. _____
2. _____

Share your choices with others in your group, and then discuss possible leads for future training and self-study.

Summary

As Schmidt (1999) advised, "If viewed as a means of facilitating learning and involvement rather than diminishing human interaction, technology can become an asset"

(p. 319). This chapter has offered some possible resources, considerations, and applications that can contribute to humanizing technology so that learning and involvement are maximized. School counselors must determine how to balance a technological world with the human touch.

References

Harris-Bowlsby, J., Dikel, M. R., & Sampson, J. P. (1998). *The internet: A tool for career planning.* Columbus, OH: National Career Development Association.

Naisbitt, J. (1982). *Megatrends: Ten new directions transforming our lives.* New York: Warner Books.

Schmidt, J. J. (1999). *Counseling in schools: Essential services and comprehensive programs.* Needham Heights, MA: Allyn & Bacon.

Reflections on Chapter 13

1. How satisfied are you with your group's knowledge and skill regarding the Internet?

2. How satisfied are you with your own knowledge and skill regarding the Internet?

3. What concerns do you still have about the use of technology in counseling?

4. How do you feel about your role in developing your group's knowledge and information about the use of technology in counseling?

5. What questions do you have for yourself, your group, or your group facilitator?

6. Notes:

✚ Chapter 14
Synthesis

In Chapter 3, we challenged you to remain objective as you explored some of the facets of systems thinking. This entire handbook has asked you to see the big picture and then to analyze its component parts as you participated in the exercises in each chapter. Now it is important for you to put the pieces back together again. We are confident that what you see will look more complete now.

In this chapter, three activities are provided to help you synthesize the content of the entire handbook. By reexamining your group's original flowchart, making a school board presentation, and then reviewing the process that completes the facilitation of your group's task, you should be at a point where you can integrate the most essential elements of a comprehensive developmental school guidance and counseling program.

Activity 14.1   Revisiting the Flowchart

Individually, take a few minutes to review the flowchart your group created in Chapter 3. Then, discuss the following questions:

1. How did you use the flowchart in setting the direction for your group's actions?

2. In what ways has your flowchart evolved into a more refined product?

3. How did the flowchart help in accomplishing your group's tasks?

4. What are some differences in how various members of your group used flowcharting to conceptualize all or parts of the program?

5. How will you use the flowchart in your group's school board presentation?

Activity 14.2 The School Board Presentation

Now is the time for you to package your plan and sell it to the school board. To do this, we suggest you go back and review key messages from the previous chapters. For example, in Chapter 1, we asked you to reflect on "meaningful information." What information do you believe will be most meaningful to a school board?

Remember which roles you were to play with the planning groups. Try to represent those roles to the school board. How will you tap people's strengths and talents? You may want to videotape your presentation.

Consider how long a typical (major) school board presentation lasts. As you plan your presentation, try to stay within that same time frame. How much can the board members take in during one presentation? What do you want them to remember most about your presentation? What about the learning styles of school board members?

If this is a real presentation to a real school board, this may be your one opportunity to shine. We suggest that you conduct a practice run. Be sure that each of you knows what you will say and how you will present it. Use materials and resources that you know will influence the board members positively. A Power Point presentation can be quite persuasive.

If this is an in-class activity, as one of the class groups is presenting its program model, one of the other class groups should act as a school board. As you are playing the role of a school board member, you need to consider certain political possibilities. Pause for a moment and visualize what a school board member might be looking for in such a presentation. Try to think like a school board member. Help the members of the group that is giving the presentation face some of the realities of making a school board presentation. Although the temptation will be great at times, try not to "overdo" the role-playing; just make it as real as possible.

After you have made your presentation, write down observations on the following topics:

1. The best part of our group's presentation was:

2. An important question raised by the board was:

3. How I felt about my individual part in the presentation:

4. Items in our plan that may need further attention:

5. What I learned about making school board presentations:

Upon further reflection about your final product, consider the following:

1. How successful have you been in visualizing an entire guidance and counseling program? How do you know this?

2. How does your plan reflect systems thinking?

3. What was the turning point or catalyst for your group to obtain and maintain a common focus?

4. What are the special features of your plan?

5. What did the other team have in its plan that you wish you had in yours?

6. Being as objective as possible, how would you assess the technical and aesthetic quality of your final product?

7. Add any other comments about your group's final plan.

Activity 14.3 Processing the Process

One of the major aspects of the cooperative learning experience that was used to create your comprehensive developmental school counseling plan has been to thrust you into a group process that is not unlike many that you will encounter as a school counselor. Because you have been so involved in developing a *product,* you may not have been able to appreciate all the lessons that have been learned from the process. The following outline is designed to help you process the process.

1. Early in the handbook, we mentioned that you would be moving through three, and possibly four, typical stages of group process (forming, storming, norming, and performing). To what extent was this movement realized in your planning group?

4	3	2	1
Very much	To a considerable degree	Somewhat	Not at all

2. To what degree did cooperative learning contribute to the quality of your final product?

4	3	2	1
Very much	To a considerable degree	Somewhat	Not at all

3a. To what degree did you feel competition with the other groups?

4	3	2	1
Very much	To a considerable degree	Somewhat	Not at all

3b. If you felt competition, what was the source of the feeling?

3c. If School District A and School District B are given the task of designing comprehensive school counseling plans, to what degree should they cooperate in that mission?

4a. In the classroom activity, each of you was assigned a role to represent within your planning group. Although assignment of such roles is artificial, you must recognize that in the real world people with even less vision about school counseling will often fill these roles. How important was it for the planning group to keep the different role perspectives in mind in the development of your plan?

4	3	2	1
Very much	To a considerable degree	Somewhat	Not at all

4b. What was the significance of having those roles in this group process?

4	3	2	1
Very much	To a considerable degree	Somewhat	Not at all

4c. How open were you to the perceptions of people as they represented their roles?

4	3	2	1
Very much	To a considerable degree	Somewhat	Not at all

5. What "group" lessons did you learn from this project that you feel will be applicable to your work as a school counselor?

6. What "planning" lessons did you learn from this project that you feel will be applicable to your work as a school counselor?

7. What things did you discover about yourself during this group experience?

8. One of the major challenges given to you in the beginning of the course was to choose a director of school counseling. In reflecting upon this entire experience,

think about the implications of program leadership for your future. What did you learn about leadership?

On a separate sheet of paper, provide some feedback to the leader of your group. Use the following outline:

a. Things you did well:
b. Things I think you need to be aware of:
c. A comment about our final product and the role you played in its development:

Director of School Counseling: While others are providing you with feedback, write down the three most important lessons or insights you learned about leadership from your experience as this group's leader.

9. On a blank sheet of paper, write your name in bold letters at the top and circulate the paper so each member of your group can write something positive or validating about your contribution to the group and its mission.

10. Please list any other lessons learned or comments that will help you remember the essential facets of this cooperative learning experience.

Summary

You have worked diligently to produce a comprehensive developmental school counseling program model of which your group can be proud. More important, this process has empowered each of you to go out into the schools and develop such a program the right way! We are fully aware that these exercises and activities have been demanding. Some pithy statement about promises and rose gardens is a temptation here, but we know you do not want to hear it. Instead, we congratulate you on gaining important insights into the complexity and significance of team planning and focused programming.

♯ Appendix A

ASCA Role Statement: The School Counselor

The American School Counselor Association recognizes and supports the implementation of comprehensive developmental counseling programs at all levels. The programs are designed to help all students develop their educational, social, career, and personal strengths to become responsible and productive citizens. School counselors help create and organize these programs, as well as provide appropriate counselor interventions.

School counseling programs are developmental by design, focusing on needs, interests, and issues related to the various stages of student growth. There are objectives, activities, special services, and expected outcomes, with an emphasis on helping students to learn more effectively and efficiently. There is a commitment to individual uniqueness and the maximum development of human potential. A counseling program is an integral part of a school's total educational program.

THE SCHOOL COUNSELOR

The school counselor is a certified professional educator who assists students, teachers, parents, and administrators. Three generally recognized helping processes used by the counselor are counseling, consulting, and coordinating: 1) Counseling is a complex helping process in which the counselor establishes a trusting and confidential working relationship. The focus is on problem-solving, decision-making, and discovering personal meaning related to learning and development; 2) Consultation is a cooperative process in which the counselor-consultant assists others to think through problems and to develop skills that make them more effective in working with students; 3) Coordination is a leadership process in which the counselor helps organize and manage a school's counseling program and related services.

School counselors are employed in elementary, middle/junior high, senior high, and postsecondary schools. Their work is differentiated by attention to age-specific developmental stages of growth and related interests, tasks, and challenges. School counselors are human behavior and relationship specialists who organize their work around fundamental interventions.

Counselor interventions have sometimes been referred to as functions, services, approaches, tasks, activities, or jobs. They have, at times, been viewed as roles themselves, helping to create the image of the counselor. In a comprehensive developmental counseling program, school counselors organize their work schedules around the following basic interventions.

Individual Counseling

Individual counseling is a personal and private interaction between a counselor and a student in which they work together on a problem or topic of interest. A face-to-face, one-on-one meeting with a counselor provides a student maximum privacy in which to freely explore ideas, feelings, and behaviors. School counselors establish trust and build a helping relationship. They respect the privacy of information, always considering actions in terms of the rights, integrity, and welfare of students. Counselors are obligated by law to report and to refer a case when a person's welfare is in jeopardy. It is the counselor's duty to inform an individual of the conditions and limitations under which assistance may be provided.

Small Group Counseling

Small group counseling involves a counselor working with two or more students together. Group size generally ranges from five to eight members. Group discussions may be relatively unstructured or may be based on structured learning activities. Group members have an opportunity to learn from each other. They can share ideas, give and receive feedback, increase their awareness, gain new knowledge, practice skills, and think about their goals and actions. Group discussion may be problem-centered, where attention is given to particular concerns or problems. Discussions may be growth-centered, where general topics are related to personal and academic development.

Large Group Guidance

Large group meetings offer the best opportunity to provide guidance to the largest number of students in a school. Counselors first work with students in large groups wherever appropriate because it is the most efficient use of time. Large group work involves cooperative learning methods, in which the larger group is divided into smaller working groups under the supervision of a counselor or teacher. The guidance and counseling curriculum, composed of organized objectives and activities, is delivered by teachers or counselors in classrooms or advisory groups. School counselors and teachers may co-lead some activities. Counselors develop and present special guidance units which may give attention to particular developmental issues or areas of concern in their respective schools and they help prepare teachers to deliver part of the guidance and counseling curriculum.

Consultation

The counselor as a consultant helps people to become more effective in working with others. Consultation helps individuals think through problems and concerns, acquire more knowledge and skill, and become more objective and self-confident. This intervention can take place in individual or group conferences, or through staff-development activities.

Coordination

Coordination as a counselor intervention is the process of managing various indirect services which benefit students and being a liaison between school and community agencies. It may include organizing special events which involve parents or resource people in the community in guidance projects. It often entails collecting data and disseminating information. Counselors might coordinate a student needs assessment, the interpretation of standardized tests, a child study team, or a guidance related teacher or parent education program.

THE PREPARATION OF SCHOOL COUNSELORS

School counselors are prepared for their work through the study of interpersonal relationships and behavioral sciences in graduate education courses in accredited colleges and universities. Preparation involves special training in counseling theory related to school settings. Particular attention is giving to personality and human development theories and research, including career and life-skills development; learning theories, the nature of change and the helping process; theories and approaches to appraisal, multi-cultural and community awareness; educational environments; curriculum development; professional ethics; and, program planning, management, and evaluation.

Counselors are prepared to use the basic interventions in a school setting, with special emphasis on the study of helping relationships, facilitation skills, and brief counseling; group dynamics and group learning activities; family systems; peer helper programs; multi-cultural and cross-cultural helping approaches; and educational and community resources for special school populations.

School counselors are aware of their own professional competencies and responsibilities within the school setting. They know when and how to refer or involve other professionals. They are accountable for their actions and participate in appropriate studies and research related to their work.

RESPONSIBILITY TO THE PROFESSION

To assure high quality practice, counselors are committed to continued professional growth and personal development. They are active members of the American Counseling Association, formerly the American Association for Counseling and Development, and the American School Counselor Association, as well as state and local professional organizations which foster and promote school counseling. They also uphold the ethical and professional standards of these associations.

School counselors meet the state certification standards and abide by the laws of the states where they are working. Counselors work cooperatively with individuals and organizations to promote the overall development of children, youth, and families in their communities.

Source: American School Counselor Association. (1990). Role statement: The school counselor. Alexandria, VA: Author. Reprinted with the permission of the American School Counselor Association.

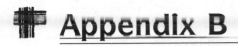

Appendix B

School Counselor Competencies

PERSONAL CHARACTERISTICS OF EFFECTIVE COUNSELORS

The personal attributes or characteristics of school counselors are very important to their success. Effective counselors usually

- have a genuine interest in the welfare of others.
- are able to understand the perspective of others.
- believe individuals are capable of solving problems.
- are open to learning.
- are willing to take risks.
- have a strong sense of self-worth.
- are not afraid to make mistakes and attempt to learn from them.
- value continued growth as a person.
- are caring and warm.
- possess a keen sense of humor.

SCHOOL COUNSELOR COMPETENCIES

School counselors must know various theories and concepts (knowledge competencies) and must be able to utilize a variety of skills (skill competencies). Further, they must be competent professionals and effective persons. The competencies needed by today's counselors are presented below.

Knowledge Competencies

School counselors need to *know*

- human development theories and concepts
- individual counseling theories
- consultation theories and techniques
- family counseling theories and techniques
- group counseling theories and techniques
- career decision-making theories and techniques

- learning theories
- motivational theories
- the effect of culture on individual development and behavior
- evaluation theories and processes
- ethical and legal issues related to counseling
- program development models

Skill Competencies

School counselors should be able to demonstrate *skills* in

- diagnosing student needs
- individual counseling
- group counseling
- consultation with staff, students, and parents
- coordination of programs, e.g., testing, career development, substance abuse
- career counseling
- educational counseling
- identifying and making appropriate referrals
- administering and interpreting achievement, interest, aptitude, and personality tests
- cross-cultural counseling
- ethical decision-making
- building supportive climates for students and staff
- removing and/or decreasing race and gender bias in school policy and curriculum
- explaining to the staff, community, and parents, the scope of practice and functions of a school counselor
- planning and conducting inservice for staff
- identifying resources and information related to helping clients
- evaluating the effectiveness of counseling programs

Professional Competencies

School counselors should be able to

- conduct a self-evaluation to determine their strengths and areas needing improvement
- develop a plan of personal and professional growth to enable them to participate in lifelong learning
- advocate for appropriate state and national legislation
- adopt a set of professional ethics to guide their practice and interactions with students, staff, community, parents, and peers

Source: American School Counselor Association. (1990). *School counselor competencies.* Alexandria, VA: Author. Reprinted with the permission of the American School Counselor Association.

Appendix C

ASCA Position Statement: The School Counselor and Developmental Guidance

THE POSITION OF THE AMERICAN SCHOOL COUNSELOR ASSOCIATION (ASCA)

Developmental guidance should be an integral part of every school counseling program and be incorporated into the role and function of every school counselor.

The Rationale

During recent years a number of counselor educators and school counselors have advanced the proposition that counseling can and should be more proactive and preventive in its focus and more developmental in its content and process. Viewed in the context of evolving societal emphasis upon personal growth and an expanding professional expertise, developmental guidance has resulted in a potentially dynamic and promising approach to the helping relationship of the school counselor. Developmental guidance is a reaffirmation and actualization of the belief that guidance is for all students and that its purpose is to maximally facilitate personal development.

There are several general principles which should help insure quality and effectiveness in the implementation of developmental guidance:

1. The program should be systematic, sequential, and comprehensive.
2. The program should be jointly founded upon developmental psychology, educational philosophy, and counseling methodology.
3. Both process and product (of the program itself and the individuals in it) should be stressed.
4. All the personal domains—cognitive, affective, behavioral, experiential, and environmental—should be emphasized.

5. Programs should emphasize preparation for the future and consolidation of the present.
6. Individualization and transfer learning should be central to program procedure and method.
7. Evaluation and corrective feedback are essential.

Source: American School Counselor Association. (1984). *Position statement: The school counselor and developmental guidance.* Alexandria, VA: Author. Reprinted with the permission of the American School Counselor Association.

Appendix D

The School Counselor and Comprehensive School Counseling Programs

THE POSITION STATEMENT OF THE AMERICAN SCHOOL COUNSELOR ASSOCIATION (ASCA)

ASCA endorses comprehensive school counseling programs that promote and enhance student learning. The focus of the program is on the three broad and interrelated areas of student development: academic, career, and personal/social development. Each encompasses a variety of desired student learning competencies, which form the foundation of the developmental school counseling program. The school counselor uses a variety of activities and resources to promote the desired student development. School counselor responsibilities include organization, implementation, and coordination of the program.

The Rationale

A comprehensive school counseling program is developmental in nature. It is systematic, sequential, clearly defined, and accountable. The foundation of the program is developmental psychology, educational philosophy, and counseling methodology. Proactive and preventative in focus, the school counseling program is integral to the educational program. It assists students in acquiring and using life-long skills through the development of academic, career, self-awareness, and interpersonal communication skills. The goal of the comprehensive school counseling program is to provide all students with life success skills.

The school counseling program has characteristics similar to other educational programs, including a scope-and-sequence; student competencies or outcomes; professionally credentialed personnel; materials and resources; and national standards for evaluation.

We recognize that our educational system is being challenged by the increasing needs of today's students and the rising expectations of society. Many of our children enter school with emotional, physical, or interpersonal barriers to learning. Although comprehensive school counseling programs include necessary crisis-oriented responsive services, the emphasis is on developmental skill building for all students beginning when students enter school and continuing as they progress through the grades.

Effective school counseling programs are a collaborative effort between the counselor and other educators to create an environment which promotes school success. Staff and counselors value and respond to the diversity and individual differences in our society and communities. Comprehensive school counseling programs help ensure equal opportunities for all students to participate fully in the educational process.

This school counseling model is compatible with the *National Education Goals* and the *National Standards for School Counseling Programs*.

The Counselor's Role

Within a comprehensive school counseling program, counselors will focus their skills, time, and energy on direct service to students, staff, and families. ASCA recommends a maximum counselor-student ratio to be 1:300. School counselors will spend 20% of their time in direct service to students. Indirect services will include counseling program planning, maintenance and evaluation, participation in school site planning and implementation, partnerships and alliances with postsecondary institutions, businesses and community agencies, and other tasks which enhance the mission of the program.

The comprehensive school counseling program balances many components. It requires counselors to deliver individual and small group counseling and large group guidance; to teach skill development in academic, career, and personal/social areas; to provide consultation and case management; and to coordinate, manage, and evaluate the school counseling program.

As student advocates, school counselors participate as members of the educational team. They consult and collaborate with teachers, administrators, and families to assist students to be successful academically, vocationally, and personally. School counselors are indispensable partners with the instructional staff in the development of contributing members of society. They assure, on behalf of students and their families, that all school programs facilitate the educational process and offer the opportunity for school success.

Summary

A written comprehensive, developmentally-based pre-K–12 school counseling program should be implemented in every school district. It should include a systematic and planned program delivery that productively involves all students and promotes and enhances the learning process.

The comprehensive school counseling program facilitates student development in three areas:

- academic development, which includes the acquisition of skills, attitudes, and knowledge which contributes to effective learning in school and throughout the life-span;
- career development, which includes the foundation for acquisition of skills, attitudes, and knowledge which will enable students to make a successful transition from school to careers;

- personal/social development which includes the acquisition of skills, attitudes, and knowledge to help students understand and respect self and others, acquire effective interpersonal skills, understand and practice safety and survival skills, and develop into contributing members of society.

The comprehensive school counseling program should be supported by appropriate resources and implemented and coordinated by a credentialed professional school counselor.

Source: American School Counselor Association. (1997). *The school counselor and comprehensive school counseling programs*. Alexandria, VA: Author. Reprinted with the permission of the American School Counselor Association.

Appendix E

American School Counselor Association Ethical Standards for School Counselors

Revised June 25, 1998

PREAMBLE

The American School Counselor Association (ASCA) is a professional organization whose members have a unique and distinctive preparation, grounded in the behavioral sciences, with training in counseling skills adapted to the school setting. The school counselor assists in the growth and development of each individual and uses his or her specialized skills to protect the interests of the counselee within the structure of the school program. School counselors subscribe to the following basic tenets of the counseling process from which professional responsibilities are derived:

- Each person has the right to respect and dignity as a human being and to counseling services without prejudice as to person, character, belief, or practice regardless of age, color, disability, ethnic group, gender, race, religion, sexual orientation, marital status, or socioeconomic status.
- Each person has the right to self-direction and self-development.
- Each person has the right of choice and the responsibility for goals reached.
- Each person has the right to privacy and thereby the right to expect the counselor-counselee relationship to comply with all laws, policies, and ethical standards pertaining to confidentiality.

In this document, ASCA has specified the principles of ethical behavior necessary to maintain and regulate the high standards of integrity, leadership, and professionalism among its members. The Ethical Standards for School Counselors were developed to clarify the nature of ethical responsibilities held in common by school counseling professionals. The purposes of this document are to:

- Serve as a guide for the ethical practices of all school counselors regardless of level, area, population served, or membership in this professional Association;
- Provide benchmarks for both self-appraisal and peer evaluations regarding counselors' responsibilities to students, parents, colleagues and professional associates, schools and communities, as well as to one's self, and the counseling profession; and
- Inform those served by the school counselor of acceptable counselor practices and expected professional behavior.

A.1. RESPONSIBILITIES TO STUDENTS

The professional school counselor:

a. Has a primary obligation and loyalty to the student, who is to be treated with respect as a unique individual.

b. Is concerned with the educational, career, emotional, and behavioral needs and encourages the maximum development of each counselee.

c. Refrains from consciously encouraging the counselee's acceptance of values, lifestyles, plans, decisions, and beliefs that represent the counselor's personal orientation.

d. Is responsible for keeping informed of laws, regulations, and policies relating to counselees and strives to ensure that the rights of students are adequately provided for and protected.

A.2. Confidentiality

The professional school counselor:

a. Informs the counselee of the purposes, goals, techniques, and rules of procedure under which she/he may receive counseling assistance at or before the time when the counseling relationship is entered. Disclosure notice includes confidentiality issues such as the possible necessity for consulting with other professionals, privileged communication, and legal or authoritative restraints. The meaning and limits of confidentiality are clearly defined to counselees through a written and shared disclosure statement.

b. Keeps information confidential unless disclosure is required to prevent clear and imminent danger to the counselee or others or when legal requirements demand that confidential information be revealed. Counselors will consult with other professionals when in doubt as to the validity of an exception.

c. Discloses information to an identified third party who, by her or his relationship with the counselee, is at high risk of contracting a disease that is commonly known to be communicable and fatal. Prior to disclosure, the counselor will ascertain that the counselee has not already informed the third party about his or her disease and he/she is not intending to inform the third party in the immediate future.

d. Requests of the court that disclosure not be required when the release of confidential information without a counselee's permission may lead to potential harm to the counselee.

e. Protects the confidentiality of counselee's records and releases personal data only according to prescribed laws and school policies. Student information maintained in computers is treated with the same care as traditional student records.

f. Protects the confidentiality of information received in the counseling relationship as specified by federal and state laws, written policies, and applicable ethical standards. Such information is only to be revealed to others with the informed consent of the counselee, consistent with the obligation of the counselor as a professional person. In a group setting, the counselor sets a norm of confidentiality and stresses its importance, yet clearly states that confidentiality in group counseling cannot be guaranteed.

A.3. Counseling Plans

The professional school counselor:

works jointly with the counselee in developing integrated and effective counseling plans, consistent with both the abilities and circumstances of the counselee and counselor. Such plans will be regularly reviewed to ensure continued viability and effectiveness, respecting the counselee's freedom of choice.

A.4. Dual Relationships

The professional school counselor:

avoids dual relationships which might impair her or his objectivity and increase the risk of harm to the client (e.g., counseling one's family members, close friends, or associates). If a dual relationship is unavoidable, the counselor is responsible for taking action to eliminate or reduce the potential for harm. Such safeguards might include informed consent, consultation, supervision, and documentation.

A.5. Appropriate Referrals

The professional school counselor:

makes referrals when necessary or appropriate to outside resources. Appropriate referral necessitates knowledge of available resources and making proper plans for transition with minimal interruption of services. Counselees retain the right to discontinue the counseling relationship at any time.

A.6. Group Work

The professional school counselor:

screens prospective group members and maintains an awareness of participants' needs and goals especially in relation to the goals of the group. The counselor takes reasonable precautions to protect members from physical and psychological harm resulting from interaction within the group.

A.7. Danger to Self and Others

The professional school counselor:

informs appropriate authorities when the counselee's condition indicates a clear and imminent danger to the counselee or others. This is to be done after careful deliberation and, where possible, after consultation with other professionals. The counselor informs the counselee of actions to be taken so as to minimalize his or her confusion and to clarify counselee and counselor expectations.

A.8. Student Records

The professional school counselor:
maintains and secures records necessary for rendering professional services as required by laws, regulations, institutional procedures, and confidentiality guidelines.

A.9. Evaluation, Assessment, and Interpretation

The professional school counselor:

a. Adheres to all professional standards regarding selecting, administering, and interpreting assessment measures. The counselor recognizes that computer-based testing programs require specific training in administration, scoring, and interpretation which may differ from that required in more traditional assessments.
b. Provides explanations of the nature, purposes, and results of assessment/evaluation in language the counselee(s) can understand.
c. Does not misuse assessment results and interpretations and takes reasonable steps to prevent others from misusing the information.
d. Uses caution when utilizing assessment techniques, making evaluations, and interpreting the performance of populations not represented in the norm group on which an instrument is standardized.

A.10. Computer Technology

The professional school counselor:

a. Promotes the benefits of appropriate computer applications and clarifies the limitations of computer technology. The counselor ensures that (1) computer applications are appropriate for the individual needs of the counselee; (2) the counselee understands how to use the application; and (3) follow-up counseling assistance is provided. Members of underrepresented groups are assured equal access to computer technologies and the absence of discriminatory information and values within computer applications.
b. Counselors who communicate with counselees via internet should follow the NBCC Standards for WebCounseling.

A.11. Peer Helper Programs

The professional school counselor:
has unique responsibilities when working with peer helper programs. The school counselor is responsible for the welfare of counselees participating in peer programs under his or her direction. School counselors who function in training and supervisory capacities are referred to the preparation and supervision standards of professional counselor associations.

B. RESPONSIBILITIES TO PARENTS
B.1. Parent Rights and Responsibilities

The professional school counselor:

   a. Respects the inherent rights and responsibilities of parents for their children and endeavors to establish, as appropriate, a cooperative relationship with parents to facilitate the counselee's maximum development.

   b. Adheres to laws and local guidelines when assisting parents experiencing family difficulties that interfere with the counselee's effectiveness and welfare.

   c. Is sensitive to cultural and social diversity among families and recognizes that all parents, custodial and noncustodial, are vested with certain rights and responsibilities for the welfare of their children by virtue of their role and according to law.

B.2. Parents and Confidentiality

The professional school counselor:

   a. Informs parents of the counselor's role, with emphasis on the confidential nature of the counseling relationship between the counselor and counselee.

   b. Provides parents with accurate, comprehensive, and relevant information in an objective and caring manner, as is appropriate and consistent with ethical responsibilities to the counselee.

   c. Makes reasonable efforts to honor the wishes of the parents and guardians concerning information that he/she may share regarding the counselee.

C. RESPONSIBILITIES TO COLLEAGUES AND PROFESSIONAL ASSOCIATES
C.1. Professional Relationships

The professional school counselor:

   a. Establishes and maintains professional relationships with faculty, staff and administration to facilitate the provision of optimal guidance and counseling services. The relationship is based on the counselor's definition and description of the parameters and levels of his or her professional roles.

   b. Treats colleagues with professional respect, courtesy, and fairness. The qualifications, views, and findings of colleagues are represented to accurately reflect the image of competent professionals.

   c. Is aware of and optimally utilizes related professions and organizations to whom the counselee may be referred.

C.2. Sharing Information with Other Professionals

The professional school counselor:

   a. Promotes awareness and adherence to appropriate guidelines regarding confidentiality; the distinction between public and private information; and staff consultation.

   b. Provides professional personnel with accurate, objective, concise and meaningful data necessary to adequately evaluate, counsel, and assist the counselee.

c. If a counselee is receiving services from another counselor or mental health professional, the counselor, with client consent, will inform the other professional and develop clear agreements to avoid confusion and conflict for the counselee.

D. RESPONSIBILITIES TO THE SCHOOL AND COMMUNITY

D.1. Responsibilities to the School

The professional school counselor:

a. Supports and protects the educational program against any infringement not in the best interests of counselees.

b. Informs appropriate officials of conditions that may be potentially disruptive or damaging to the school's mission, personnel, and property while honoring the confidentiality between the counselor and counselee.

c. Delineates and promotes the counselor's role and function in meeting the needs of those served. The counselor will notify appropriate school officials of conditions which may limit or curtail her or his effectiveness in providing programs and services.

d. Accepts employment only for those positions for which he/she is qualified by education, training, supervised experience, state and national professional credentials, and appropriate professional experience. Counselors recommend that administrators hire only qualified and competent individuals for professional counseling positions.

e. Assists in developing: (1) curricular and environmental conditions appropriate for the school and community; (2) educational procedures and programs to meet the counselee's developmental needs; and (3) a systematic evaluation process for comprehensive school counseling programs, services and personnel. The counselor is guided by the findings of the evaluation data in planning programs and services.

D.2. Responsibilities to the Community

The professional school counselor:
collaborates with agencies, organizations, and individuals in the school and community in the best interest of counselees and without regard to personal reward or remuneration.

E. RESPONSIBILITIES TO SELF

E.1. Professional Competence

The professional school counselor:

a. Functions within the boundaries of individual professional competence and accepts responsibility for the consequences of his or her actions.

b. Monitors personal functioning and effectiveness and does not participate in any activity which may lead to inadequate professional services or harm to a client.

c. Strives through personal initiative to maintain professional competence and keep abreast of professional information. Professional and personal growth are ongoing throughout the counselor's career.

E.2. Multicultural Skills

The professional school counselor:

understands the diverse cultural backgrounds of the counselees with whom he/she works. This includes, but is not limited to, learning how the school counselor's own cultural/ethnic/racial identity impacts her or his values and beliefs about the counseling process.

F. RESPONSIBILITIES TO THE PROFESSION
F.1. Professionalism

The professional school counselor:

a. Accepts the policies and processes for handling ethical violations as a result of maintaining membership in the American School Counselor Association.
b. Conducts herself/himself in such a manner as to advance individual ethical practice and the profession.
c. Conducts appropriate research and reports findings in a manner consistent with acceptable educational and psychological research practices. When using client data for research or for statistical or program planning purposes, the counselor ensures protection of the individual counselee's identity.
d. Adheres to ethical standards of the profession, other official policy statements pertaining to counseling, and relevant statutes established by federal, state and local governments.
e. Clearly distinguishes between statements and actions as a private individual and those made as a representative of the school counseling profession.
f. Does not use his or her professional position to recruit or gain clients, consultees for her or his private practice, seek and receive unjustified personal gain, unfair advantage, sexual favors, or unearned goods or services.

F.2. Contribution to the Profession

The professional school counselor:

a. Actively participates in local, state and national associations which foster the development and improvement of school counseling.
b. Contributes to the development of the profession through the sharing of skills, ideas and expertise with colleagues.

G. MAINTENANCE OF STANDARDS

Ethical behavior among professional school counselors, Association members and non-members, is expected at all times. When there exists serious doubt as to the ethical behavior of colleagues, or if counselors are forced to work in situations or abide by policies which do not reflect the standards as outlined in these *Ethical Standards for School Counselors*, the counselor is obligated to take appropriate action to rectify the condition. The following procedure may serve as a guide:

1. The counselor should consult confidentially with a professional colleague to discuss the nature of the complaint to see if she/he views the situation as an ethical violation.

2. When feasible, the counselor should directly approach the colleague whose behavior is in question to discuss the complaint and seek resolution.

3. If resolution is not forthcoming at the personal level, the counselor shall utilize the channels established within the school, school district, the state SCA, and ASCA Ethics Committee.

4. If the matter still remains unresolved, referral for review and appropriate action should be made to the Ethics Committees in the following sequence:
   - state counselor association
   - national counselor association

5. The ASCA Ethics Committee functions for educating—and consulting with—the membership regarding ethical standards. The Committee periodically reviews and recommends changes in code. The Committee will also receive and process questions to clarify the application of such standards. Questions should be submitted in writing to the ACA Ethics Chair. Finally, the Committee will handle complaints of alleged violations of our ethical standards. Therefore, at the national level, complaints should be submitted in writing to the ASCA Ethics Committee, c/o the Executive Director, American School Counselor Association, 801 North Fairfax, Suite 310, Alexandria, VA 22314.

H. RESOURCES

School counselors are responsible for being aware of, and acting in accord with, standards and positions of the counseling professions as represented in official documents such as those listed below.

American Counseling Association. (1995). *Code of ethics and standards of practice.* Alexandria, VA (5999 Stevenson Avenue, Alexandria, VA 22034) 1 800 347 6647 www.counseling.org.

American School Counselor Association. (1997). *The national standards for school counseling programs.* Alexandria, VA (801 North Fairfax Street, Suite 310, Alexandria, VA 22314) 1 800 306 4722 www.schoolcounselor.org.

American School Counselor Association. (1998). *Position statements.* Alexandria, VA.

American School Counselor Association (1998). *Professional liability insurance program.* (Brochure). Alexandria, VA.

Arredondo, Toperek, Brown, Jones, Locke, Sanchez, and Stadler. (1996). Multicultural counseling competencies and standards. *Journal of Multicultural Counseling and Development.* Vol. 24, No. 1. See American Counseling Association.

Arthur, G. L., and Swanson, C. D. (1993). *Confidentiality and privileged communication.* See American Counseling Association.

Association for Specialists in Group Work. (1989). *Ethical guidelines for group counselors.* Alexandria, VA. See American Counseling Association.

Corey, G., Corey, M. S., and Callanan. (1998). *Issues and Ethics in the Helping Professions.* Pacific Grove, CA: Brooks/Cole. (Brooks/Cole, 511 Forest Lodge Rd., Pacific Grove, CA 93950) www.thomson.com.

Crawford, R. (1994). *Avoiding counselor malpractice.* Alexandria, VA. See American Counseling Association.

Forrester-Miller, H., and Davis, T. E. (1996). *A practitioner's guide to ethical decision making.* Alexandria, VA. See American Counseling Association.

Herlihy, B., and Corey, G. (1996). *ACA ethical standards casebook.* Alexandria, VA. See American Counseling Association.

Herlihy, B., and Corey, G. (1992). *Dual relationships in counseling.* Alexandria, VA. See American Counseling Association.

Huey, W. C., and Remley, T. P. (1988). *Ethical and legal issues in school counseling.* Alexandria, VA. See American Counseling Association.

Joint Committee on Testing Practices. (1988). *Code of fair testing practices in education.* Washington, DC: American Psychological Association (1200 17th Street, NW, Washington, DC 20036) 202 336 5500

Mitchell, R. W. (1991). *Documentation in counseling records.* Alexandria, VA. See American Counseling Association.

National Board of Certified Counselors. (1998). *National board of certified counselors: Code of ethics.* Greensboro, NC (3 Terrace Way, Suite D, Greensboro, NC 27403-3660) 336 547 0607 www.nbcc.org.

National Board of Certified Counselors. (1998). *Standards for the ethical practice of webcounseling.* Greensboro, NC.

National Peer Helpers Association. (1989). *Code of ethics for peer helping professionals.* Greenvilee, NC (PO Box 2684, Greenville, NC 27836) 919 522 3959 nphaorg.aol.com.

Salo, M., and Schumate, S. (1993). *Counseling minor clients.* Alexandria, VA. See American School Counselor Association.

Stevens-Smith, P., and Hughes, M. (1993). Legal issues in marriage and family counseling. Alexandria, VA. See American School Counselor Association.

Wheeler, N. and Bertram, B. (1994). *Legal aspects of counseling: Avoiding lawsuits and legal problems.* (Videotape). Alexandria, VA. See American School Counselor Association.

Ethical Standards for School Counselors was adopted by the ASCA Delegate Assembly, March 19, 1984. The first revision was approved by the ASCA Delegate Assembly, March 27, 1992. The second revision was approved by the ASCA Governing Board on March 30, 1998 and adopted on June 28, 1998.

Source: From American School Counselor Association, Alexandria, VA, 1998. Reprinted with permission.

Index

TO THE OWNER OF THIS BOOK:

We hope that you have found *Developing Your School Counseling Program: A Handbook for Systemic Planning* useful. So that this book can be improved in a future edition, would you take the time to complete this sheet and return it? Thank you.

School and address: _____

Department: _____

Instructor's name: _____

1. What I like most about this book is: _____

_____

_____

2. What I like least about this book is: _____

_____

_____

3. My general reaction to this book is: _____

_____

_____

4. The name of the course in which I used this book is: _____

_____

5. Were all of the chapters of the book assigned for you to read? _____

   If not, which ones weren't? _____

   _____

6. In the space below, or on a separate sheet of paper, please write specific suggestions for improving this book and anything else you'd care to share about your experience in using the book.

_____

_____

_____

OPTIONAL:

Your name: _____ Date: _____

May we quote you, either in promotion for *Developing Your School Counseling Program: A Handbook for Systemic Planning* or in future publishing ventures?

Yes: _____ No: _____

Sincerely yours,

Zark VanZandt
Jo Hayslip